STUDIES IN HISTORY, ECONOMICS AND PUBLIC LAW

Edited by the
FACULTY OF POLITICAL SCIENCE
OF COLUMBIA UNIVERSITY

Number 556

THE THEORY OF FLUCTUATIONS IN CONTEMPORARY ECONOMIC THOUGHT

BY

SIDNEY D. MERLIN

THE
THEORY OF FLUCTUATIONS
IN
CONTEMPORARY ECONOMIC
THOUGHT

BY

SIDNEY D. MERLIN, Ph. D.

New York
COLUMBIA UNIVERSITY PRESS

To

The Memory of My Father

PREFACE

THE present study, made possible by a Social Science Research Council Award in 1946, was undertaken with considerable trepidation because its range is wide, much of the subject matter is controversial, and the methodological issues which form an important part of the subject seem remote from real problems.

My interest centered initially on an even broader question which I pondered over a long period in the government service: namely, the relationship between economic theory and economic policy, in particular the treatment of policy problems as "non-economic," as outside the scope of economic science proper. I came to feel that the theories of economic fluctuations and employment which grew out of the ferment of the thirties threw an altogether different light on this relationship; and that they were worth exploring on these as well as other grounds.

I should like to acknowledge my debt to Professor J. M. Clark for many helpful suggestions which improved this book substantially. To Professor Frederick C. Mills I am grateful for advice and encouragement given when most needed. Professors Moses Abramovitz, James W. Angell, Joseph Dorfman, Carter Goodrich and William S. Vickrey read the manuscript in an early draft and kindly gave me the benefit of their comments. I wish especially to thank Mrs. C. A. Stewart, of the Department of Economics, for helping me so efficiently over obstacles that try the soul of an author.

I owe more than I can say to my wife both for her patience while I was occupied in writing this book during many evenings and weekends and for her assistance in editing the manuscript. I am solely responsible for the views presented in these chapters and for errors which may remain.

S. D. M.

SILVER SPRING, MARYLAND
SEPTEMBER, 1948

CONTENTS

	PAGE
PREFACE	7

CHAPTER I

Introduction	11

CHAPTER II

A Survey of the Main Theories	16
The Background	16
The Theories Summarized	20
Hicks' Dynamics	21
Keynes' Theory of Employment	22
Swedish Dynamic Theory	25
Econometric Theory of the Cycle	27
Some Implications of the Theories	30

CHAPTER III

Price Instability and the Theory of Demand	35
The Problem of Persistence and Change in Economic Theory	35
Temporary Equilibrium Analysis	42
The Concept of Expectations	52

CHAPTER IV

The Influence of Swedish Sequence Analysis	59
The Theory of the Cumulative Process	60
The Unit-Period	66
A Note on Methodology	71
Conclusion	76
Addendum: The Concept of Fluctuations in Econometric Analysis	79

CHAPTER V

Dynamic Factors in Keynesian Theory	91
Changes in Total Output	94
Long-Term Expectations	98
Keynes on the Trade Cycle	105
Keynesian Business Cycle Theory	109
Short-Run versus Long-Run Factors in Investment Activity	114

10 CONTENTS

CHAPTER VI

Employment and the Demand for Capital 121

    Some Long-Term Factors Governing Employment 123
    The Short-Run Background 131
    The Question of Investment Outlets 139

CHAPTER VII

Some Implications and Conclusions 145

    A Note on the Equilibrium Concept 145
    Economic Fluctuations and the Dynamic Problem 153

Bibliography 163

Index 167

CHAPTER I

INTRODUCTION

ALTHOUGH employment today is at record levels, the fear of depression and unemployment still confronts us. The eyes of a troubled world are turned toward the United States, questioning whether this country can maintain its economy at high levels of activity, or whether it will again plunge downward into large-scale unemployment and economic contraction. World affairs hang in the balance. The problem of unemployment in a private enterprise economy is obviously of more than academic interest, but it is to the economic theorists and students of economic relations that we must turn for precise, if not conclusive, analysis of the problem.

Business fluctuations and unemployment have become problems of increasing importance in economic theory. The concern of economists with these problems is reflected in the literature on economic dynamics which assumed major proportions in the years following the depression of the thirties. In fact, the rise of dynamic theory seemed to mark a new phase of economic thought, one that promised to bring an end to the gap between business cycle theory and general theory. For the major thesis of contemporary dynamic theory, in contrast to the notion of self-righting adjustment in static theory, is that the economic system is not necessarily or inherently stable, and that the main causes of instability are to be sought within the economic system itself. Consequently in this study we shall limit ourselves almost entirely to theories of economic fluctuations developed since the early thirties around different versions of the dynamic problem.

Despite a substantial change in outlook, most of the leading theories which have been advanced over the past fifteen years in explanation of business fluctuations and unemployment remain equilibrium theories. Professor Hicks, for example, has attempted to integrate the theory of money with traditional price analysis in a theory of price movements for the economy at large. In the case of Keynesian theory, the analysis of " output as a whole " rests on a modified version of the equilibrium relations. Here some of the traditional concepts —marginal productivity and supply and demand—have been developed, in combination with monetary effects and the consumption function, into a theory of underemployment equilibrium. Of the theories considered in this study, only those of the Swedish economists break with equilibrium analysis in the traditional sense.

The present study examines the bearing of dynamic theory and dynamic concepts on the notion of equilibrium. It would seem that contemporary dynamic theory has qualified traditional equilibrium analysis in an important respect. In equilibrium analysis determinate relations are postulated—what Marshall, in loose parlance, referred to as " enough, and only enough, premises for . . . conclusions "—meaning the factors which govern supply and demand decisions and their intersection at the set of prices which make supply equal to demand. In dynamic theory an attempt is made to bring factors formerly regarded as indeterminate within the scope of equilibrium analysis. These factors relate to estimates of the future made by individual firms and consumers, when prices and the data change, and to the process of (supply and demand) adjustment undertaken on the basis of such estimates. More generally, dynamic theory deals with economic variables relating to different points of time and with hypotheses regarding casual connections between such variables.

The inclusion of these factors brings the limiting assumptions of equilibrium reasoning into full view. We find that the introduction of dynamic factors makes it difficult to maintain the notion of determinate relations and smooth adjustments to changes in the data. For one thing, in dynamic theory the field of study is changes in the economy at large, changes in which the process of adjustment may affect the data of the problem. The reactions of firms and consumers to changes in prices and in the data are linked not merely to changes in relative prices but to changes in the price level (Hicks); not to changes in individual outputs alone, but to changes in output as a whole (Keynes). Here the data are not independent of the process of adjustment. When the data change, adjustments by firms as a whole and by consumers as a whole may involve appreciably secondary changes in the data; and once we admit that the data may not stay put *during the process of adjustment*, the analytical conditions necessary to determine equilibrium prices no longer hold. Instead of adjustments to the data at some fixed level of economic activity, we may have cumulative movements in which adjustments to changes in the data induce further changes in the data, which result in further adjustments, etc. Dynamic theory takes us into treacherous terrain where the data are constant and yet not constant, where we catch glimpses of the disturbing impact of institutional and technical changes. The dynamic system is on the edge of instability and cumulative movement.

The main thesis advanced in this study is that attempts to develop a theory of cyclical (or other) fluctuations from a modified equilibrium analysis leave fluctuations in employment and prices unexplained. The view that the economic system is not necessarily or inherently stable because of uncertainty about the future movement of prices and profits is a considerable advance over the notion of " frictions " in economic statics. The properties of money are dominating here because money provides the vital link between present and future. It is through money that the (subjective) uncertainty associated with " the accumulation of wealth for an indefinitely postponed future " [1] is registered on decisions made in the present. Yet the tenor of the theories examined here is that the economic system conforms to an equilibrium tendency and that business fluctuations take place around this equilibrium.

1 J. M. Keynes " The General Theory of Employment," *Quarterly Journal of Economics*, February, 1937, p. 213.

A complete or adequate explanation of disturbances within the context of equilibrium analysis does not seem possible. The dynamic properties of money are intended to provide this explanation through the action of price (and profit) expectations. Thus expectations as to future prices (and profits) are based on estimates of future supply and demand conditions which are translated into current decisions to hold or spend money. But the experience of prices—i. e. conditions of demand and supply—in the immediate past is not a sufficient basis for an explanation of expectations. Expectations are conditioned by factors not contained in the analysis of price equilibrium and, insofar as their causation is sought in price experience alone, are indeterminate. We find ourselves traversing the circular relationships of equilibrium analysis without being able to come to grips with the fundamental, originating causes of business fluctuation. It becomes necessary in fact to allude to forces existing outside the price system which may influence expectations and make the system liable to fluctuations. Furthermore, the term " fluctuations " in contemporary theory generally refers to short-run, irregular movements, rather than cyclical changes. On the whole, the movements studied in current dynamic theory are non-periodic, marginal changes which result in (small) oscillations around a shifting equilibrium; not the great upheavals which may occur against the background of chronic imbalance of the economic system.

Much has been said to qualify traditional theory when it is admitted that forces within the economic system may produce fluctuations and that " equilibrium " is not synonymous with the full employment of resources. On the other hand, equilibrium analysis seems to obscure the nature of such forces because the latter suggest relationships which lie outside the traditional equilibrium scheme. However, the purpose of the present study is not primarily one of criticism, but is rather an endeavor to isolate some of the principal forces which govern business fluctuations and to inquire how they may be brought into theoretical analysis. The theories discussed here will be sifted for their contribution to an understanding of this problem.

This brief study cannot hope to do justice to the many outstanding achievements which mark the development of dynamic theory and business cycle discussion over the past two or three decades. The theories discussed are recent contributions and are still controversial. For this reason, perhaps, they may be fairly representative of the range of contemporary dynamic theory. Above all, they represent the furthermost stage of advance in the attempt to integrate traditional theory and the problem of economic fluctuations.

In referring to traditional theory in what follows, Professor R. F. Harrod's useful definition may be kept in mind. Commonly accepted theory is divided by Professor Harrod into " general theory " and its specialized branches, although, as he notes, there is no authorized version of " general theory." The latter consists

> primarily of a number of functional equations expressing individual preference schedules and a number of identities, such as that supply must be equal to demand and the elucidation of such questions as whether there are as many equations as there are unknowns and whether the solutions are single or multiple. The result of these enquiries should make it clear whether the equilibrium of the system as a whole is stable or unstable or undetermined, whether there are alternative positions of equilibrium, etc. . . . Within the corpus of the general theory may be included the formulation of the market conditions that are required for the realization of some kind of maximum. . . . In contrast with the theory of value in this very general form, may be set the special theories formulated to deal with specific problems such as interest, profit, joint production, discriminating monopoly, etc.[2]

2 R. F. Harrod, " Mr. Keynes and Traditional Theory," *Econometrica,* January, 1937, pp. 74-75.

CHAPTER II
A SURVEY OF THE MAIN THEORIES

THE depression of the thirties saw a ferment of ideas without parallel in the main stream of economic thought since the days of Ricardo, Malthus, and West. Traditional theory, which had for so long identified the business cycle with frictions acting on a self-righting mechanism,[1] was faced by events which flatly contradicted its major thesis and threatened its breakdown. This is not the place for an inquiry into the reasons which made the great depression of the thirties a leavening force in economic thought, for there have been other depressions of great magnitude and intensity. The reasons are manifold and complex, and only separate study could do the subject justice. Under the pressure of critical events, economists had to seek new moorings. Ideas which had been developing outside traditional analysis, growing doubts about the efficacy of traditional theory, and the experience of the depression and its aftermath —all these converged in the search for an adequate theoretical explanation of business cycle (or other) fluctuations. In the period that followed the depression of the thirties we have witnessed the substantial growth of dynamic theory and the first concerted attempt to make business cycle theory an integral part of theoretical analysis.

THE BACKGROUND

Until the middle of the nineteenth century, business cycles were commonly regarded as temporary disturbances of the " normal course " of events which presented no serious theoretical problems. Ricardo gave business crises passing attention

---

1 There were a number of illustrious exceptions, among them Wicksell, Veblen, Mitchell, and J. M. Clark, who did not accept the notion of "frictions." But their views filtered slowly into traditional economic thought and received due recognition only after the re-appraisal which came in the thirties.

when he referred to the " temporary reverses and contingencies, produced by the removal of capital from one employment to another."[2] The causes of crises mentioned by Ricardo range from changes in consumer taste to new taxes and the effects of a war, changes which only divert trade momentarily from its usual channels. Business depressions in the experience of the classical economists from Smith to Mill seemed to be associated with speculative booms, wars, and technical changes — a range of extraordinary causes lying outside the area of their economic science.[3]

Despite criticism of Say's Law of Markets by Malthus, Sismondi, Marx, and others, it was not until the regularity of the business cycle was established in the second half of the nineteenth century by a number of independent investigators—John Mills, Lord Overston, W. Langton, and others—that fluctuations in business activity came to be viewed as something more than exceptional deviations from the smooth course of events. Even then it was still customary to explain business fluctuations in terms of the action of outside factors on a self-contained system of economic relations, rather than by economic causes. W. S. Jevons' theory of the cycle laid the originating causes to periodic fluctuations in sun radiation and sought its economic effects in corresponding variations in the price of corn and other agricultural products. This conception of the business cycle— not Jevons' particular version, but the notion that the periodicity of the cycle is caused by non-economic factors—drew increasing criticism from factual investigators such as Clement Juglar, Tugan-Baranovski, and others. But business cycle problems were given no systematic attention in standard economic treatises—in the works of Marshall and his followers and

2 David Ricardo, *The Principles of Political Economy and Taxation* (New York: E. P. Dutton & Co., 1911), p. 175.

3 The classical tendency to associate extraordinary events with business crises has been discussed by F. E. Trautmann. *Cf.* Simon Kuznets' " Equilibrium Economics," *Quarterly Journal of Economics*, May, 1930, p. 382.

among the Lausanne and other Continental theorists. Wicksell's studies, which drew in part on Austrian sources, and dealt with the factors governing the balance between savings, investment, and productive activity, exerted little influence outside the Scandinavian countries for a number of years. Early in the present century Veblen did indeed advance an embryonic theory of the cycle based on the conflict between " business and industrial employments ", namely the recurrent deflation of capital values resulting from the progress of industrial technique. While Veblen's views profoundly influenced American economic thought, they did not seriously modify or displace traditional notions.

In 1913 W. C. Mitchell gave the problem of business cycles its most comprehensive empirical treatment to date. Although influenced by Veblen's distinction between pecuniary and industrial employments, as well as his theory of the cycle, Mitchell was not concerned with the relation between business cycle theory and traditional theory. His study—" an analytic description of the complicated processes " of the business cycle—took note of the complexity of the problem, listed a number of prevailing theories, and examined in a wealth of detail the interrelated stages of development of the cycle. Despite this and other advances in empirical investigation of the business cycle, the relation of traditional theory to business cycle theory remained undeveloped except for Schumpeter's *Theory of Economic Development* which appeared shortly after Mitchell's study.

The cleavage between economic theory and the facts developed in business cycle research continued even during the twenties when the significance of business cycle study for theoretical economics was becoming more and more evident. A number of German economists, among them Von Loewe, Lederer, and Carrel, did attempt to state the relation between pure theory and business cycle theory and to develop the outlines of a dynamic economics. But their work remained fragmentary and incomplete. In a study which confirmed his earlier views, Mitchell, during the same period, indicated the challenge which business cycle research posed for traditional theory. However, he was not concerned with reconciling the two. " Hence it is no part of my task," he wrote, " to determine how the fact of cyclical oscillations in economic activity can be reconciled with the general theory of equilibrium, or how that theory can be reconciled with facts." [4] Instead, as earlier, he confined himself to an " analytic description " and felt it more helpful to treat the problem " in terms of the relations among a number of complex variables, rather than in terms of cause and effect." [5] In his work on overhead costs, J. M. Clark further developed the principle of acceleration which he had advanced in 1917—namely, the hypothesis that demand for producers goods is influenced by the rate of change in demand for finished goods and that fluctuations in demand for finished goods tend to induce intensified fluctuations in producers goods industries. Despite its dynamic features and the advance it represented over current discussions of the cycle in terms of " frictions ", Clark's work, too, remained outside the scheme of traditional theory as a cogent commentary on its limitations and as an anticipation of things to come.

With the onset of the great depression and in the period that followed, the relation of business cycle theory to traditional analysis assumed new importance in economic thought. Under the pressure of social and economic events, the development of a dynamic analysis which would explain business fluctuations and unemployment as part of the economic system, rather than as a consequence of " frictions ", became one of the main concerns of economic theorists. The articles on business cycle theory brought together under one cover by a committee of the American Economic Association are illustrative.[6] While more recent

4 W. C. Mitchell, Business Cycles, vol. I, *The Problem and Its Setting* (New York: National Bureau of Economic Research, 1927), p. 462.

5 *Ibid.*, p. 471.

6 Readings in Business Cycle Theory, The American Economic Association (Philadelphia: The Blakiston Co., 1944).

articles relating to business cycle theory may have been emphasized, the fact remains that among those contained in the volume only three of seventeen were written prior to the thirties. Instead of scattered writings by a few leading students of the cycle, the period following the great depression is characterized by a voluminous literature forming the contributions of many persons—contributions concerned largely with the theoretical import of the business cycle. Indeed, the feature that distinguishes the work of theoretical economists from the thirties on is a new emphasis on processes of instability in the system of private enterprise and the way in which this instability is to be systematically interpreted in economic theory.

The Theories Summarized

Several principal theories have emerged in recent years which aim at an explanation of unemployment and the intimately related problem of cyclical (or other) fluctuations in a private enterprise economy. While they overlap in certain respects, fundamentally these theories represent distinct views of the problem. The theories summarized here have been chosen because of their importance in advancing dynamic theory and the analysis of economic fluctuations.

The feature that these theories have in common is their attempt to explain how money links present economic decisions with the future. Yet the theory of money has developed from two independent lines of thought:[7] cash balance analysis and capital analysis. The first, or cash balance approach, stems from Walras. Although Walras did discuss the difference between money as a medium of exchange on the one hand and the utility of money on the other, he did not develop the significance of money as a link between the present and the future. The notion of cash balances and its relation to the problem of uncertainty was developed after Walras, mainly by Laving-

---

7 *Cf.* Rosenstein-Rodan, "The Coordination of the General Theory of Money and Prices," *Economica*, August, 1936, pp. 270-273.

ton, Cannan, and Hawtrey. As the theory of general price adjustment under the influence of uncertainty, cash balance analysis in recent years has been given more exact form by Myrdal, Hicks, and Lange. Capital analysis as a second approach to the role of money had early forerunners in Bentham, H. Thornton, Malthus, and Joplin. It was developed more systematically by Knut Wicksell, and later by Hayek, Keynes, Lindahl, Myrdal, Ohlin, and others. In capital analysis the problem of the influence of money on the supply and demand for commodities in the traditional sense gives way to a related but different sort of concern: the effect of monetary changes on prices and production in the capital goods and consumer goods industries and on (aggregate) investment and national income. These two main divisions of the theory of money have persisted in the contemporary theories studied here and have contributed substantially to differences of interpretation and emphasis.

HICKS' DYNAMICS

One of the leading contemporary theories is that developed by Professor Hicks in *Value and Capital*. Hicks endeavors to adapt the traditional theory of price formation in the market to the problem of economic fluctuations. The basic approach is that of Walrasian equilibrium analysis with certain additional features: prices at any given time are determined if tastes, resources and the state of technique are given; " rules of change " are developed for a system of temporary equilibrium altering from period to period as the plans made by individual consumers and firms change; and plans in a given period depend both on current and expected prices. Hicks attempts to develop a theory of fluctuations from the theory of price by viewing goods, money, and securities as substitutes. The stability of the price system depends on the effect of differing elasticities of expectations on substitution relations—relations which either act to make supply greater than demand when prices in a given market rise, and so induce stabilizing forces which tend to reduce prices, or which fail to make supply greater than demand and initiate cumulative price rises. If individuals, for example, expect that prices in the future will rise proportionately less than current prices are rising (inelastic expectations), consumers will postpone purchases by substituting money for goods and producers will postpone input and increase output, thus tending to make supply greater than demand. On the other hand, if individuals expect that prices in the future will rise proportionately more than current prices are rising (elastic expectations), expenditures will be shifted from the future to the present by substituting goods for money and current demand will be increased. Under these conditions producers will increase input and postpone output, the total effect being to increase prices and to start a cumulative price rise. A cumulative movement occurs then if supply does not exceed demand when current prices rise, or demand exceed supply when current prices fall. When securities as well as money and commodities become possible substitutes the substitution relation is more complex; but the result in terms of expectations that make for stability or instability is substantially the same.

While Hicks attempts to analyze cumulative movements of the price system, his theory of temporary equilibrium relates only to changes over the short-run—the " week " or any other convenient period of time in which the stock of capital resources and the other data are given. Moreover the concept of expectations which is intended to explain changes in prices and output through the substitution relations between goods, money, and securities deals with possible oscillations around full-employment equilibrium. Finally, Hicks develops the possibility of cumulative (upward or downward) price movements when expectations are " elastic ", but he does not provide us with a theory of the business cycle or even a complete theory of (irregular) fluctuations in output and employment.

KEYNES' THEORY OF EMPLOYMENT

Keynesian theory, with its schedule relations between the marginal efficiency of capital, the propensity to consume, and the rate of interest, relations which together determine the level of employment and national income, represents a distinct type of theory. While Keynesian theory in its original form provides an analysis of equilibrium at less than full-employment, rather than a theory of fluctuations in employment, it does contain a number of dynamic elements, among them the concept of the multiplier and the marginal efficiency of capital. The notion of time periods is rather fundamental to the relation between an (incremental) addition to investment, the resulting increase in income and the subsequent effect on consumption and savings. Though the analysis in the General Theory of Employment is aimed at relations existing at a point in time, the income-consumption relation expressed in the multiplier has been developed in dynamic terms and used as the basis of a theory of fluctuations by Harrod, Hansen, Samuelson, and others. In Keynes' analysis, moreover, the schedule of the marginal efficiency of capital serves as a link between present and future. It is the "prospective yield of capital" and changing views about the future which, relative to the cost and scarcity of capital assets, influence the scale of investment and the volume of employment.[8]

Keynes himself evidently conceived of the General Theory as a partial approach to dynamic analysis achieved through the concept of long-term expectations. But he closely interwove his discussion of dynamic factors with his analysis of the equilibrium level of employment and thereby added to the difficulty of cataloguing his theory exclusively as statics or dynamics. For example, he employs the concept of long-term expectations in order to trace the influence of the future on the marginal efficiency of capital and on the existing equilibrium. Yet Keynes refers to his chapter on long-term expectations as "a digression ... on a different level of abstraction from most of this book." [9] Again, in his summary of the General Theory,

8 J. M. Keynes, *The General Theory of Employment, Interest and Money* (New York: Harcourt Brace and Co., 1936), pp. 141-145.

9 *Ibid.*, p. 240.

Keynes mentions a number of special characteristics of his independent variables " which are not logically necessary ", in his view, to an analysis of underemployment equilibrium. Here he speaks of the " economic system in which we live " as " subject to severe fluctuations in respect of output and employment ", although " not violently unstable ". In his brief discussion of the cycle at still another point, it is the sharp reversal of long-term expectations which is responsible for the collapse in the marginal efficiency of capital and the turning point in the cycle.[10] Keynes, it seems, attempted an analysis of underemployment equilibrium in which one of his main determining variables, the marginal efficiency of capital, can be fully explained only by causal forces not contained in his equilibrium analysis—forces which can produce fluctuations. His theory of employment gains in reality, but his equilibrium analysis loses its determinate qualities.

The combination of static and dynamic elements in Keynes' General Theory may possibly be explained by the fact that he was attempting to advance a short-run analysis of shifting equilibrium which, like Marshall's, takes note of the long run but does not succeed in incorporating some of its most important features in the relations given at a point of time. These relations, in fact, assume constancy of " the other things ", including the stock of capital goods. Long-term inequality of wealth and income [11] and the secular decline in the marginal efficiency of capital [12] provide the background for Keynes' theory of employment. But the " prospective yield of capital " is too slender a concept to explain how long-run changes may be affecting investment over the short-run. In all due respect to Keynes, it must be added that he was not primarily concerned with economic dynamics or with the question of business fluctuations. Rather, despite fairly frequent reference to

10 *Ibid.*, p. 316.

11 *Ibid.*, pp. 31, 219, Chapter 244.

12 *Ibid.*, p. 307.

dynamic features, he was concerned foremost with the forces which determine "the actual employment of the available resources" and with bringing the "influence of money" within the scope of "the general theory of supply and demand".

SWEDISH DYNAMIC THEORY

Dynamic theory has been substantially advanced by the distinction, made by the Swedish economists, between ex ante and ex post income, investment, and savings. The Swedish economists have been included in this discussion because, while their work has been fundamental to the development of dynamic theory in recent years, it cannot be classified as equilibrium analysis in the traditional sense and presents some significant points of contrast with the other theories discussed in this study.

The economists of this group—Lindahl, Ohlin, Lundberg—are in general agreement with Keynes' attempt to link together the theories of price, money, and employment. But they take issue with "orthodox equilibrium constructions" and with Keynes' equilibrium analysis on the grounds that Keynes' central concepts, in particular the relation between volume of consumption and realized income, hold only at the end of a period. Keynes did not make use of the notion of periods and his theory of employment rests on ex post concepts—concepts which describe realized magnitudes instead of expected magnitudes. Actually, "planned investment" will differ from planned saving "unless they should happen to be equal by mere chance."[13] At the end of a period income, investment, and saving during that period are usually found to be different from what they were expected to be; and a dynamic explanation requires an analysis of the effect of differences between expected and actual events on expectations and plans in subsequent periods. This criticism of Keynes' theory of employment is also directed at the shortcomings of Keynes' theory of expectations. In Keynes' theory, long-term expectations, which dominate the

13 Bertil Ohlin, "The Stockholm Theory of Savings and Investment," Readings in Business Cycle Theory, op. cit., p. 126.

marginal efficiency of capital, can change erratically. As the result of ignorance of the future, expectations may depend on "whim, sentiment, or chance ", the " political and social atmosphere ", the " state of confidence ", and " fluctuations in business psychology ".

On the other hand, in Swedish process analysis the important factors — the factors which have causal significance for economic action—are not realized (ex post) magnitudes, but expected (ex ante) magnitudes which explain economic plans and actions for a series of periods extending into the future. The ex post " registration " of transactions in terms of income and expenditure, summed for all firms and individuals, describes what has happened in a past period and indicates the degree to which plans and expectations have or have not been realized. Discrepancies between planned magnitudes at the end of a period, for example, between planned saving and planned investment, induce adjustments which lead to new plans and expectations for the following periods. It is this combination of ex ante and ex post events that may be regarded as the cause of a process. In Ohlin's words,

> after a description of actual events during a certain finished period, and of the differences between these events and the expectations which existed at the beginning of the period, follows an account of those expectations for the future which more or less govern actions during the next period. The registration of events during this second period reveals again that expectations do not all come true, a fact which influences expectations and actions during the third period, etc.[14]

In Swedish process analysis, the development of actual transactions in relation to plans and expectations is studied in terms of reactions having different time-sequences and time-lags, for example, the speed with which profit and other income expectations are affected, the speed with which the amounts of cash

14 *Ibid.*, p. 94.

in the hands of different firms and individuals are changed and so on. This is basically a theory of psychological causation: it is the " speed of the psychological reactions which is the governing factor ".[15] The Swedish economists make a serious attempt to gauge reaction patterns and " speeds of reaction " in terms of changes in economic quantities like income, investment, and employment. But the actual character of expectations and their effect on plans—the factor having the decisive causal role—are unknown and can only be treated schematically.

ECONOMETRIC THEORY OF THE CYCLE

The econometric theorists—Frisch, Tinbergen, Haavelmo, Koopmans, and others—have attempted to develop in exact terms the conditions which must be satisfied in dynamic equilibrium. The general dynamic problem is viewed as that of explaining a relation among (economic) variables located at different points in time. " Speeds of reaction " and lags [16] are introduced as in Swedish process analysis, but these relations are subjected to empirical check. Thus once a problem has been stated in rigorous functional terms, the causal relations involved are tested by measurements on the time series in which pertinent variables occur. Variables are not restricted to a fixed scheme as in general equilibrium theory or in Keynesian analysis. Instead " explanatory " variables are selected to fit each of a number of economic problems. On the whole, however, the work of the econometricians has produced a method, rather than a theory of business fluctuations.

---

15 *Ibid.*, p. 105.

16 By " speeds of reaction " and lags are meant the time required for adjustments among economic quantities when changes occur, or when, in a particular relationship, there is a lag between cause and effect. For example, the rate at which prices, quantities and interest rates adjust to a fall in actual income and expected incomes and affect the level of investment, or the rate at which other prices adjust to price changes in a particular commodity market.

Dynamic relations are approached in terms of equilibrium analysis. A (functional) equation relating the variable to be explained to the "explanatory" variables is first developed. Structural relations consisting of numerical values for constant ("influencing") coefficients and lags are then introduced into the equation. "Influencing" coefficients, for example, may be given elasticities of supply and demand, or other constants which indicate the quantitative reaction in the relation between the variables of an equation. The equation of relationship includes, in addition, so-called "non-systematic" terms, i. e. that part of the change in a variable which is attributable to accidental causes, changes in government policy, strikes, inventions, and other "new" events which cannot be predicted. These causes of change in the variables to be explained are to be distinguished from the "systematic" causes included in the "explanatory" variables and structural relations.[17] A determinate system of equations is postulated when there are *n* equations and *n* variables—the familiar condition of equilibrium in which the number of equations equals the number of unknowns. Although this is an equilibrium scheme, the system of equations given by the structural relations and non-systematic terms is supposed to develop, or evolve, from certain initial conditions. As Frisch puts it, " The essential character of a set of equations that is dynamic . . . is, indeed, that it does not *lock* the system (does not stop motion) although it is determinate (i. e., although it contains the same number of equations as unknowns)."[18]

This method of analysis has been applied by econometricians in testing theories of the business cycle.[19] Its principal purpose

17 See Chapter IV, p. 80, this study.

18 Ragnar Frisch, "On the Notion of Equilibrium and Disequilibrium," *Review of Economic Studies*, February, 1936, pp. 100-101.

19 For example, Tinbergen, *Statistical Testing of Business Cycle Theories*, Vol. I: A Method and its Application to Investment Activity, and II: Business Cycles in the United States of America, 1919-1932.

is to provide a systematic basis for the quantitative measurement of economic relationships and for a rigorous mathematical statement of the conditions which define such relationships.
In defining the conditions of the dynamic problem, however,
econometric analysis has also provided a generalized theory of
fluctuations. In fact, Ragnar Frisch presented a theory of the
cycle in an early statement of the econometric approach.[20]

The possibility of explaining fluctuations in the analysis advanced by the econometricians arises from sudden changes in
the so-called " unsystematic terms " in the equations of relationship. When an unforeseen change occurs which was not contained in the equations of relationship, e. g., a strike, a political
change, an invention—the system defined by the equations is
disturbed. " If the disturbance takes the form of a discontinuous (or nearly) discontinuous change in initial conditions,"
writes Frisch, " as these were determined by the previous evolution of the system, or in the form of the structural equations,
we call it a shock." [21] Frisch terms the evolution of the structural equations the " propagation problem ", or the element that
determines the length of cycles and the tendency towards damping. The impact of irregular " impulses " from outside this system prevents its damping and determines the intensity of the
fluctuations. Thus irregular disturbances acting on a dynamic
system may produce more or less regular fluctuations. This
places the source of continuing fluctuations outside the economic system.

Frisch also suggested that the irregular disturbances which
act on an oscillating, but " rigidly determined ", economic
system might possibly be regarded as chance (random) factors.
The problem of random variables has been developed extensively in econometric analysis since Frisch's statement of the
shock theory of the cycle. The attempt has been made to define

20 Ragnar Frisch, *Economic Essays in Honor of Gustav Cassel, Propagation Problems and Impulse Problems in Dynamic Economics.*

21 Ragnar Frisch, *op. cit.*, p. 102.

probability conditions for the " non-systematic " variables in econometric analysis, despite the fact that economic time series do not rigorously obey the laws of statistical probability. The notion of functionality—the mutual interdependence of the variables in a system—should give us equations of causal connection which closely approximate observed relations. Roughly speaking, " random variables " represent the (estimated) gap between theory and observation. From the econometric point of view the concept of " random variables " is needed to develop complete functional models and determinate dynamic systems. To the extent that the forces impounded in " random variables " are systematic forces, rather than purely chance forces, this method may conceal causal factors of some importance to the problem of economic fluctuations. Yet, in their work on " random variables " the econometricians have supplied a much-needed statement of the rigorous conditions which must be fulfilled when economic relations are put into functional form. They have suggested in addition the price that must be paid for a rigid functional analysis of the dynamic problem.

SOME IMPLICATIONS OF THE THEORIES

To revert to Professor Harrod's usage, modern developments in theory have had a revolutionary effect on the specialized branches of accepted theory. There is, for example, no separation of interest, investment, and profit theory in the theory of employment and in current dynamic analysis. The theory of money has been removed from the niche it occupied as " monetary theory " and incorporated in a theoretical treatment which includes the level of savings and investment corresponding to a given level of prices and output or a given level of supply and demand. As Ohlin has observed, this is tantamount to dropping the assumption of " monetary stability " in traditional price and distribution analysis. " Through some such assumption," notes Ohlin, " all other causes of incomplete employment than those connected with monopoly—including monopolistic trade union

policy—and ' frictions ' are ruled out, as well as movements
in the general price levels." [22] In conventional price theory it
is assumed that particular changes, say, in the supply and demand for a given commodity, are either instantaneous or do
not have sufficiently large repercussions on the price system to
warrant consideration of variations in national income and total
output and price levels. If the assumption of monetary stability
is dropped, changes in small segments of the price system, for
example in particular commodity markets, can be studied for
their effect on general processes of expansion and contraction
of total employment and national income.

Changes in total employment and income, however, are not
explained merely by dropping the assumption of monetary
stability. A truly dynamic theory should provide an explanation
of the causal relation between monetary changes and changes
in total employment and national income. With the exception
of the process analysis developed by the Swedish economists,
who are on the whole critical of equilibrium analysis, the
dynamic theories which have been discussed here do not adequately explain how changes in " output as a whole " are
brought about. In Professor Hicks' analysis, for example,
changes in saving, investment, and output may occur when
equilibrium price in a particular market changes. It is the elasticity or inelasticity of expectations as to price and other factors,
especially the type of substitution relations they induce, that
determines whether equilibrium is restored or cumulative price
increases or price decreases take place. In Keynes' analysis there
can be no disequilibrium because every change in investment is
followed by an automatic adjustment of income, consumption,
and saving to the new level of investment. It is an equilibrium
analysis in which changes in the marginal efficiency of capital,
leading to a new equilibrium level of employment, depend on
changes in other factors not directly contained in the analysis,

22 Ohlin, *op. cit.*, p. 119.

namely the state of long-term expectations.[23] The fluctuating and precarious nature of long-term expectations exercises a restraining effect on investment;[24] and, through their influence on the marginal efficiency of capital, expectations are a determining, though frequently implicit, element of the equilibrium level of employment. Though Keynes and Hicks employ different causal explanations, in each case equilibrium depends on the state of expectations and changes in expectations. But in neither case are changes in expectations actually explained by or contained in the equilibrium analysis itself. Expectations are psychological variables for which no complete causal explanation is given in Hicks' system of temporary equilibrium or in Keynes' theory of employment.

The fact that expectations and chance (random) influences are not clearly defined in dynamic theory is traceable perhaps to the attempt to approach dynamic problems through equilibrium analysis. When a set of interdependent causal forces has been isolated and all other forces are then held constant, the forces selected as causal are supposed to determine the unknowns and the equilibrium if the number of equations equals the number of unknowns. The domain of traditional theory is marginal analysis within the short-run. When the attempt is made to extend equilibrium analysis to cover dynamic problems, the chain of causation cannot be held to the customary boundaries of statics but must be traced back in order to explain changes in the conditions held constant in traditional theory. Individuals respond to changes in the data by revising their estimates of the data and their holdings of cash, securities or goods (Hicks). Or changes in profit-expectations, coupled with the propensity to hoard and a given level of consumption, lead to changes in the marginal efficiency of capital and the scale of investment and employment (Keynesian theory). Or the effects (say) of a change in crops

23 Keynes, *op. cit.*, pp. 246-247.
24 *Ibid.*, pp. 153, 162.

(data) on the volume of employment, prices, and other economic variables is studied (econometric theorists). We tend to get a series of short-run equilibria when the relations linking the periods together (supply and demand, prices, costs, profits, etc.) carry over from one period to the next. Fluctuations arise from sudden changes in the relations which held in past periods, namely through altered estimates of the future (elastic price expectations or a break in profit expectations) or through the impact of chance disturbances. But the reason for abrupt (discontinuous) changes in relations which held in the past is not explained. They are attributed to shifts in business psychology and in the subjective interpretation of the future which cannot be accounted for by the equilibrium analysis proper. In making chance disturbances the source of fluctuations, the econometric theorists likewise suggest causal factors not accounted for in their basic analysis.

In conclusion, the dynamic theories developed during and after the onset of the depression of the thirties attempt to explain how instability may arise within the system of private enterprise. These theories study the impact of disturbances on an equilibrium system; and instability of the economic system is defined in terms of the disruption of an equilibrium (price or employment) position which may end in cumulative expansion or contraction. But it is not explained why revision of expectations will sometimes lead to a new equilibrium position and at other times to cumulative expansion or contraction of the economic system. Indeed the sources of disturbance appear in large part to lie outside the scheme of supply and demand relations and of prices which form the subject matter of equilibrium analysis. In fact, as far as can be judged, according to several of the theories discussed in this study, the economic system may be open to irregular disturbances resulting from almost any conceivable set of forces acting through expectations. Furthermore, these theories do not explain turning points in a process of cumulative expansion or contraction of the economic system. The forces which govern turning points, as well as the fundamental originating causes of fluctuations, are not explained.

The gap between business cycle theory and general theory — the treatment of economic fluctuations for so long as " frictions " acting on a self-righting mechanism—was, then, hardly an oversight of the economic theorists or an historical accident corrected by the experience of the great depression. Rather, the gap between the two seems to have been a con‑ sequence of the short-term equilibrium analysis which formed the basis of theoretical inquiry, an analysis which has been perpetuated in contemporary dynamic theory and its treatment of fluctuations. While the contemporary theories deal with the instability of prices and employment in a system of private enterprise, the forces which may generate instability remain obscure and undefined.

CHAPTER III
PRICE INSTABILITY AND THE THEORY OF DEMAND

THE closely related problems of unemployment and cyclical (or other) fluctuations—problems that lie outside the immediate scope of traditional theory—have become, for most economists, the significant questions in economic theory and policy. Yet equilibrium analysis has been retained in a number of the theories which have been advanced since the thirties to explain unemployment and fluctuations in business activity. Two wholly different ideas seem to be joined together in these theories: upward movements that reverse themselves, reach a minimum point and reverse themselves again; and the position of rest which may be displaced by disturbances. The first is a process that does not reach a position of rest but alternates between upward and downward movements, either irregularly or with some degree of regularity, in which case we may refer to the movements as cyclical. The second implies a balance of forces which is restored by corrective adjustments when the balance is upset. The notion of a balance of forces has a very specific meaning in equilibrium analysis and the term " balance " does not necessarily signify " equilibrium " in the conventional sense. Equilibrium means that special set of prices which is compatible with the maximum positions (in terms of utility and profit) of all individuals in the system. The question is how are the two ideas of process and position of rest reconciled in contemporary theories of business fluctuations which make use of the equilibrium concept.

THE PROBLEM OF PERSISTENCE AND CHANGE IN ECONOMIC THEORY

As in other disciplines that aim at a systematic explanation of events, the problem of establishing persistent causal relations in economic theory requires the selection of " significant " variables and the exclusion of others. But this process of selection and elimination of variables must rest on some hypothesis for reducing the number of variables to the proportion of a workable functional scheme and holding others constant. In the so-called exact sciences, causal laws are first advanced as hypotheses. These may be checked by observations on the data and verified, modified, or replaced by other hypotheses. When a hypothesis has stood the test of confirmation by the facts, when it has been subjected to numerous observations and verified as a causal explanation, it begins to attain the status of a causal law valid within wide areas of time and space. Copernicus' hypothesis of solar revolution, further development of the hypothesis by Kepler and Galileo, and Newton's confirmation and synthesis in his laws of motion is a classic example. But the process of empirical verification through which these laws were developed depends on a particular feature of the data: the fact that physical phenomena remain relatively stable over time. Hypotheses in the exact sciences become accepted as laws when repeated observations *on relatively unchanging data* reveal persistent causal relations, relations which can be predicted from a law with known margins of error.

The experimental method of the exact sciences is closely connected with statistical procedure and with the theory of probability. Thus the empirical test of a hypothesis is the degree of correlation between hypothesis and observed events. If the deviations between hypothesis and observations, measured in terms of statistical constants, fall within a preassigned range of error given by probability theory, the hypothesis is regarded as valid within this range of error. If predictions made on the basis of a hypothesis repeatedly fall within a given margin of error when checked against observations, the hypothesis tends to become accepted as a law. The use of probability theory in assigning the degree of error between hypothesis and observations depends on the statistical assumption of constancy of universes: observations are independent of each other (i. e, are random) and follow an "unchangeable law of distribution". The relative stability of observations over time—the persistence of a statistical distribution of the observations as measured by the element of chance in probability theory—makes it possible to verify hypotheses by controlled experiment in the exact sciences.

Traditional economic theory attempts to express "laws" or persistent tendencies through the equilibrium concept. Equilibrium analysis follows the assumption that resources in the hands of individuals as well as wants and techniques are independent variables and that the data, or "other things", are constant. Within this scheme, individuals (firms and consumers) attempt to maximize the return from their scarce resources by equating the allocation of resources among different uses at the margin. When supply and demand are equal for each commodity in the economic system, we have that special set of (equilibrium) prices which is compatible with the maximum positions of all individuals in the system. The main feature of the analysis is its attempt to answer the question: is the system of supply and demand equations in stable or unstable or undetermined equilibrium. A determinate (price) equilibrium is supposed to be given when the number of equations equals the number of unknowns.[1]

In isolating the variables which determine price equilibrium, traditional theory thus makes a number of simplifying assumptions. This is not an unusual procedure in the exact sciences. But unlike the hypotheses developed in the exact sciences, the causal explanation of price formation in traditional theory is

---

1 By "determinate" we mean more broadly the assumption that there is an unique solution to the relations expressed between dependent and independent variables in different types of economic problems, i. e. a dependent variable takes values which change in accordance with changes in the values of given independent variables. For example, the notion that the national income is uniquely given by the relation between the marginal efficiency of capital, the rate of interest, and the propensity to consume at a point in time represents a determinate statement. Traditional equilibrium analysis is merely one type of determinate analysis.

not readily subject to empirical verification. Probability theory is not entirely applicable to the type of observations that can be made in economics and in the social sciences generally. Observations occur in time series that include secular trends on which are overlaid seasonal patterns, cyclical movements and shorter term oscillations — a variety of intermingled changes, both uniform and irregular, for which there is no exact counterpart in the physical sciences. Observations are not independent of each other (i. e. are not random) and their distributions may change radically over time. Under these conditions a series of observations may not conform to the expected distribution within a range of error given by probability theory. Even if it were possible to postulate the stability of statistical constants derived from time series, the subjective theory of value on which the equilibrium concept rests would not be susceptible to direct measurement. The equilibrium concept may be criticized on other grounds. For example, the question whether an equilibrium is determinate involves more than equality of equations and unknowns. There may be no determinate solution to a system of equations, a situation that frequently occurs when a system of equations is not linear.[2]

As a formal system, however, equilibrium analysis is methodologically correct if the simplifying assumptions are granted. Traditional theory has made few pretensions to empirical verification; and criticism on this score may be beside the point. In fact, the conception of traditional theory as " pure theory " has fostered a practice of generalization apart from empirical reference, with the adequacy of theory to reality being judged primarily by criteria of logical consistency based on self-evident axioms about scarcity and marginal allocation. This conception of pure theory is well set forth by a comment made

---

2 We do not always know whether such equations have a unique positive solution, no solution, or several or even an infinite number of solutions. Even in the case of simple linear equations equality of the number of unknowns with the number of equations need not be a sufficient condition for determinateness.

by Keynes long before the appearance of the General Theory.
" The Theory of Economics ", observed Keynes, " does not
furnish a body of settled conclusions immediately applicable to
policy. It is a method rather than a doctrine, an apparatus of
the mind, a technique of thinking, which helps its possessor
to draw correct conclusions." [3] In commenting on this passage,
Professor Frank D. Graham has said that Keynes failed to distinguish economic theory from pure logic.[4] Yet, given the kind
of theory to which he had reference, Keynes' statement seems
unassailable.

There are, however, other than methodological objections to
the equilibrium concept. A determinate and stable price equilibrium is supposed to signify a persistent relationship between
the interdependent factors of supply and demand. If there are
small deviations away from the equilibrium position, forces are
presumably set to work which restore the equilibrium. The persistence of basic relationships implied in the concept of equilibrium is secured by definition, not by closeness of fit between
theory and observation. Yet it is this persistence that is generalized as a level toward which the economic system of reality
is supposed to return when disturbed by outside forces. Moreover, such disturbances must result from factors lying outside
the economic system. For if an equilibrium position is unstable
because of factors within the system, the supply and demand
relations cannot have the persistence which the equilibrium concept implies. The economic system then would not have a tendency to return to an equilibrium level when disturbed. Only
forces (the data) lying outside the closed interdependent system change, while the relations expressed by an equilibrium
position merely adapt to changes in the data without alteration.
Adolph Loewe has summed up this basic feature of equilibrium analysis with the statement that,

3 D. H. Robertson, *Money* (New York: Harcourt, Brace and Co., 1922),
Introduction by J. M. Keynes, p. v.

4 Frank D. Graham, *Social Goals and Economic Institutions* (Princeton
University Press, 1942), p. xvii.

equilibrium is logically bound up with the concept of a closed, interdependent system, since it is only through independence from outside influences and through the functional interconnection of the elements of the system, that the persistence of any state, i. e., of an equilibrium is achieved. We can thus say that any system of economics which operates with the concept of equilibrium must necessarily be a closed interdependent system—in short, a static system. As such the theory of movement characteristic of this system is the movement by the method of variation.[5]

That cyclical (or other) fluctuations cannot be reconciled with the notion of persistent relations expressed in traditional equilibrium analysis is well brought out by Professor Schumpeter's work on the theory of economic development, an early attempt to integrate business cycle problems and pure theory. In some ways Schumpeter's study goes much farther toward the creation of a dynamic economics than the more recent theories of cyclical (or other) fluctuations.

Schumpeter went to the heart of the problem by making a force *within* the economic system responsible for generating cyclical movements. He conceives of economic change as continuous adaptation to changes in the data as well as discontinuous movement arising from forces lodged within the economic system. He notes that,

> ... economic life changes; it changes partly because of changes in the data, to which it adapts itself. But this is not the only kind of economic change; there is another which is not accounted for by influence on the data from without, but which arises from within the system, and this kind of change is the cause of so many important economic phenomena that it seems worthwhile to build a theory for it, and, in order to do so, to isolate it from all the other factors of change ... what we are about to consider is that kind of change arising from within the system which so displaces its equilibrium point that the

5 Adolph Loewe, quoted by Kuznets, *loc. cit.*

new one cannot be reached from the old one by infinitesimal steps. Add successively as many mail coaches as you please, you will never get a railway thereby.[6]

Statics is unable to predict the consequences of discontinuous change, or to provide a basis from which a new equilibrium can be reached when the old equilibrium is completely disrupted. The task which Schumpeter sets himself is the investigation of the effect of dynamic elements in " disturbing the static equilibrium and the new equilibrium which emerges." [7]

According to Schumpeter the important factor in discontinuous change is to be found in the carrying out of " new combinations " by which he means " . . . simply the different employment of the economic system's existing supplies of productive means ".[8] The agent responsible for new combinations, the active force within the economic system making for discontinuous changes, is the rare and gifted entrepreneur who forges ahead of others in introducing new undertakings or innovations. Since they occur in " swarms ", rather than steadily, innovations provide an explanation of the discontinuous, wavelike movements that characterize economic development.

The high degree of realism attained by this theory lies in its treatment of the dynamic factors—changes in productive means —as forces arising within the economic system, not as fortuitous events acting from outside the economic system. But the standards of conduct that govern the behavior of energetic business men in this theory, the role of the entrepreneur in introducing innovations, depend on factors taken as constant. If institutional changes like industrial concentration modify or alter the function of the entrepreneur and prevent his important function of carrying out innovations, then perhaps cyclical movements may be the consequence of forces other than those suggested by

6 Joseph A. Schumpeter, *The Theory of Economic Development* (Cambridge, Massachusetts: Harvard University Press, 1934), p. 64.

7 *Ibid.*, p. 60.

8 *Ibid.*, p. 68.

Schumpeter. Schumpeter's theory introduces a single complicating factor in explanation of cycles, a factor whose causation lies in institutional changes that remain outside the scope
of pure theory. Schumpeter concludes that,

> even circumstances which do not act from without on the
> economic system as strikingly as wars or meteorological con-
> ditions must be seen from the standpoint of pure theory as
> effects of external causes of disturbances and hence in prin-
> ciple as accidental. To take an example, the sudden abolish-
> ment of protective tariffs may cause a crisis. Such a com-
> mercial measure is certainly an economic event. But we can
> assert nothing accurate about its appearance; we can only
> investigate its effects. From the standpoint of the laws of
> economic life it is simply an influence from without.[9]

His theory of economic development contains a dynamic factor
not present in traditional equilibrium analysis. Yet his theory
raises a problem similar to that encountered in the traditional
equilibrium explanation: can a relation be assumed to persist
when factors outside the closed interdependent system may
actually be causing changes in that relation?

In his later work on business cycles Schumpeter has modified the view that economic theory can be forced into closed
compartments. He has noted that it is not always possible to
determine whether a change in the institutional framework is an
" external " factor or " an act of business behavior " and that
" . . . our economic system . . . is not always describable in terms
of a logically consistent analytic model." [10]

TEMPORARY EQUILIBRIUM ANALYSIS

The economists who have attempted to adapt traditional
theory to dynamic problems have made expectations, or better
still uncertain expectations, the central concept in their analysis

9 *Ibid.*, pp. 220-221.
10 *Business Cycles* (New York: McGraw-Hill, 1939), I, 11.

of fluctuations. And money, held as a contingent form of wealth against the future, measures our "confidence" in our expectations. In Keynes' words, "our desire to hold money as a store of wealth is a barometer of the degree of our distrust of our own calculations and conventions concerning the future."[11] When the price-system is in equilibrium and price and other expectations change, cash balances are adjusted to the new situation, resulting in a movement to another equilibrium position or in disequilibrium and cumulative price movements. The attempt to develop a dynamic theory within the framework of equilibrium analysis poses a familiar question: can disturbing forces be reconciled with the notion of persistent relations implied in the equilibrium concept. Are the disturbances that may be generated by changing expectations a basic part of the price system, or are they considered to act from the outside on an interdependent set of persistent relations?

The notion of persistent relations implied in traditional equilibrium analysis has been sharply qualified in the theory of dynamic equilibrium. Instead of a static equilibrium we have an equilibrium through time—a temporary equilibrium—resulting from the fact that the data change and that anticipations are revised accordingly. Anticipations can "be correct only for a very short-run; for a longer period a part of them is bound to prove erroneous. As time passes, anticipations which proved to have been erroneous are modified; we have therefore always new data determining the new situation: an equilibrium through time ... cannot exist over more than a very short time." [12] In contrast with static equilibrium, temporary equilibrium, even when reached, may not be persistent. A much more modest notion (of the meaning) of "equilibrium" is advanced. "... by equilibrium we merely mean determinancy", write Marschak and Makower. "There is absolutely no guarantee that the

11 J. M. Keynes, "The General Theory of Employment," *Quarterly Journal of Economics*, February, 1937, p. 216.

12 P. N. Rosenstein-Rodan, *op. cit.*, p. 28 f.

(equilibrium) prices and quantities will persist through time. ... Thus prices and quantities tend to change continually, although they are determinate at each moment ".[13]

But the main problem still is the analysis of changes in equilibrium, though now in terms of the revision of anticipations as the data change. In a world where tastes, income, future prices and the size of cash purchases cannot be foreseen with perfect certainty, in short where uncertainty exists, people hold cash balances broadly interpreted as assets of all kinds. Changes in the data are met by the revision of anticipations—changed estimates of the data—which call forth corresponding adjustments in assets held and result in changes in (relative) prices.[14] " If I am right," Hicks has written, " the whole problem of applying monetary theory is largely one of deducing changes in anticipations from changes in the objective data." [15]

In this type of analysis, changes in income and investment are supposed to be continuously reflected in changes in the relative prices of factors and commodities, i. e. changes in yields and assets. There is no explicit treatment of income as a central economic variable. In fact, integration of the theory of money with price theory has produced an analysis in which there are exceedingly few references to empirical concepts. The theory of money has simply been incorporated into the theory of value, and the decisions of individuals (firms and consumers) broadened by the need for sizing up the future. The result is a theory of such generality that,

> The very concept of income can be dispensed with. ... The quantities we need are the amounts of various commodities and services consumed in various time intervals, and the asset holdings. ... To introduce the concept income would be merely

13 H. Makower and J. Marschak, "Assets, Prices and Monetary Theory," *Economica*, August, 1938, p. 270.

14 *Ibid.*, p. 287.

15 J. R. Hicks, "A Suggestion for Simplifying the Theory of Money," *Economica*, II, new series, p. 13.

to reduce the amounts consumed, and the changes in asset holdings, to a single quantity by the use of some ill-defined index numbers. For certain purposes the reduction of yields and assets to imaginary entities like consumption and investment is a useful statistical approximation. . . .

All indices are, however, only simplifications which are more or less liable to become unusable in the real world, owing to the non-uniformity of tastes and expectations, the inconstancy of the yield flow through time and its variability through time.[16]

Professor Hicks has ably systematized the theory of temporary equilibrium and adapted it to an analysis of fluctuations, specifically fluctuations in prices which may arise from changing price-expectations. Any brief discussion of its main dynamic features can hardly do justice to Hicks' complex and closely reasoned work.

Hicks summarizes the view that changing expectations may have disturbing effects when he writes as follows:

A static economy is inherently stable; small causes produce small effects; the system is therefore not liable to large disturbances, excepting those which originate definitely outside itself. But this appearance of stability was only achieved by leaving out part of the problem. As soon as we take expectations into account (or rather, as soon as we take the elasticity of expectations into account), the stability of the system is seriously weakened . . . it is not inherently and necessarily stable. It is henceforth not at all surprising that the economic system of reality should be subject to large fluctuations, nor that these fluctuations should be so very dangerous.[17]

The price system is subject to pronounced instability which exists within the economic system itself, casting doubt on the persistent relations expressed by the equilibrium concept. How

16 H. Makower and J. Marschak, *op. cit.*, pp. 284-85, 287.

17 J. R. Hicks, *Value and Capital* (1st ed.; Oxford: Oxford University Press, 1939), p. 256.

then is the notion of persistent relations brought back into the picture? How can fluctuations arise in a system in temporary equilibrium?

Professor Hicks has tried to supply the answer in an analysis directed at fluctuations in the network of market prices — fluctuations arising from changes in a single market that may, under conditions of elastic expectations, prevent restoration of equilibrium and spread to all markets. Elastic expectations can produce fluctuations for one main reason: the possibility of substituting future goods for present goods — through the interchangeability of goods, money and securities—cannot act to maintain price stability when a change in current prices changes expected prices in more than the same proportion. When consumers and entrepreneurs interpret a rise in current prices to mean a more than proportionate rise in future prices (elastic expectations), they increase expenditure and start new production by shifting from money and securities to goods. Thus, even though prices are rising, consumers draw on savings or borrow in order to buy more goods. Similarly, if, when current prices rise, producers expect that future prices for the goods they turn out will rise proportionately more, they will decrease current output, draw on cash balances (dishoard), or borrow funds in order to finance the production of goods (increased input) which can be sold in the future at higher prices. Under these conditions a rise in prices produces no adequate counteracting forces: the increase in prices does not induce the excess supply needed to meet the increased demand, and prices continue to rise. We have here a typical example of a cumulative price expansion unchecked by an excess of supply over demand or by an increase in supply which might cause prices to fall.

There is in Hicks' analysis no differentiation between capital goods and consumers goods or discussion of the relation between investment and employment. Hicks' analysis of expectations results in a theory which is concerned with general price instability and the forces which may check price instability. It is a theory of changes in the price level and the interrelation of

markets resulting from the substitution relations, based on expectations, which exist between present and future goods. It
is not a theory of fluctuations in employment in any direct
sense: employment may be assumed to fluctuate in accordance
with the correlation usually observed between price- and employ-
ment-expansion and price- and employment-contraction. That is
to say, the monetary effects of changes in expectations are not
traced through to changes in the level of investment, employment and income, but are limited to the substitution relations
existing among commodities, money, and securities and the
effect on prices.

The analysis of price formation in Hicks' system of temporary equilibrium—the system which changes from " week " to
" week "—rests on the decisions of individuals, on their behavior in making plans, in estimating the future, and in adjusting their plans as current prices and expectations change. In
an analysis centered on individual conduct, calculations of income *ex post*, writes Hicks, " are of no use to theoretical economists, who are trying to find out how the economic system
works, because they have no significance for conduct ". Income
ex post " can have no relevance to present decisions. The income which is relevant to conduct must always exclude windfall
gains. . . . Theoretical confusion between income *ex post* and
ex ante corresponds to practical confusion between income and
capital." [18] For this reason Hicks attempts to construct " a
whole general theory of economic dynamics . . . without using
the concepts of saving and income " [19] through application of
the substitution relations which exist between goods, money,
and securities. This is Hick's main contribution. His discussion

18 *Ibid.*, p. 179.

19 *Ibid.*, p. 180. Hicks does break up the response to price changes into
a substitution *and* an income effect, i. e. redistribution of income between
buyers and sellers. But the income effect is negligible where the commodity
in question plays a small part in the consumer's budget; and, as Hicks puts
it, " . . . it is only in these cases that we have a quite unequivocal law of
demand," *ibid.*, p. 32.

of the trade cycle at the close of *Value and Capital* is quite
unrelated to his main theme of dynamic changes in price levels.
By tracing the effect of changing price-expectations on decisions
to buy and sell goods, Hicks does succeed in showing that the
price system is "not inherently and necessarily stable." But
some of the main factors governing business fluctuations, like
capital accumulation, cannot be included in this type of analysis
"because they belong to a part of dynamics which falls outside
temporary equilibrium theory." [20] It is a theory of short-term
irregular price movements which does not explain how such
movements are reversed. More important still, the theory does
not really explain how stability or instability arises in terms of
price changes alone.

Hicks' analysis is subject to an even more severe restriction.
His notion of the stability conditions of exchange—i. e., that a
rise in price makes supply greater than demand, a fall in price
demand greater than supply, producing forces in each instance
which act to restore equilibrium—rests on the assumption of
perfect competition.[21] Consequently, demand-supply reactions
may not follow the path Hicks supposes if (say) reductions in
demand are accompanied by reductions in output, rather than
price, over a sizeable area of the economy. Hicks brings price-
rigidity into the picture when he considers fluctuations. But
rigid prices in his analysis are (price) stabilizing forces, not
conditions which alter the traditional scheme of supply-demand
adjustments in response to price variation.[22] If the stability conditions set forth by Hicks are indeed indeterminate in view of
widespread elements of oligopoly, then his analysis of the con-

---

20 *Ibid.*, p. 247.

21 "Under monopoly," says Hicks, "the stability conditions become indeterminate; and the basis on which economic laws can be constructed is
therefore shorn away." *Ibid.*, pp. 83-84. Hicks proposes to avoid the dilemma
by assuming "...that the markets confronting most of the firms with which
we shall deal do not differ very greatly from perfectly competitive conditions." *Ibid.*, p. 84.

22 See below.

ditions under which equilibrium is (imperfectly) stable in a dynamic system is restricted accordingly.

Hicks finds that under dynamic conditions, when expected prices affect current decisions to buy or sell goods, equilibrium may be imperfectly stable or even liable to disturbance and breakdown. But on the basis of his analysis of different elasticities of expectations, he infers that, if expectations were generally elastic, or even unity,[23] the economic system of reality would be much more unstable than it actually is. A " reasonably realistic model ...", writes Hicks, "... must give the system sufficient factors of stability to enable it to work ".[24] Consequently, Hicks concludes that possible stabilizers must exist which, when taken into account, will make his model more realistic — " elements which limit the fluctuations of the economy, though they do not prevent it from fluctuating altogether."[25] And the most important check to fluctuations, Hicks suggests, lies in price rigidities. The presence of rigid prices " means that some prices do not move upward or downward in sympathy with the rest—they consequently exercise a stabilizing influence." [26] For example, when the prices of some products rise, a general upward price-movement may be checked if there are substitute products (or factors) whose prices are rigid. We may have rigidity as a result of legislative control, monopolistic action, or because of "... lingering notions of ' just

---

23 The elasticity of a particular person's expectations is defined as the ratio of the proportional rise in expected future prices of a commodity X to the proportional rise in its current price. *Ibid.*, p. 205. If the elasticity of expectations is unity, a change in current prices will change expected prices in the same direction and proportion, and changes in price are expected to be permanent. Hicks observes, however, that "... the case where elasticities of expectations are equal to unity marks the dividing line between stability and instability. But its own stability is a very questionable sort ... the system is liable to break down at the slightest disturbance." *Ibid.*, p. 255.

24 *Ibid.*, p. 271.

25 *Ibid.*, p. 258.

26 *Ibid.*, p. 264.

price ' ".[27] Hicks suggests that wage-rates are the most important class of rigid prices because wage-rates are affected by all three types of rigidity. By working wage-rate rigidity into a scheme which assumes the existence of unemployed labor,[28] Hicks comes up with the proposition that unemployed labor is an important stabilizer when a price-expansion threatens, especially " . . . when unemployment extends to a good many sorts of labour ".[29] Indeed, since " generalized labour " has strong substitution (or transformation) relations with most types of goods, " Unemployment is the best stabilizer we have yet found." [30]

Hicks endeavors to probe more deeply into the reasons why money wages should be rigid and suggests that the explanation lies in the fact that

> those people who fix wages have some degree of confidence in a stable value of money—that is to say, because they have fairly *inelastic* price-expectations. So long as they retain the view that a certain level of prices is ' normal,' it is perfectly

27 *Ibid.*, p. 265.

28 Unity elasticity of expectations is also assumed, i. e. substitution between sorts of commodities, rather than substitution over time. Hicks sets up a relation between a rigid buyers' price and a " shadow " sellers' price where an increase in demand for a commodity cannot result in a change in price— say, if price subsidies are employed—but does result in an increase in the amount sold just as if the price had risen. Now a rise in general prices will mean a relative fall in the (rigid) buyers' price. This tends to lower the prices of all goods for which the commodity with the rigid price is a substitute, or of all goods into which it can be transformed. The direct effect of the rigid price is (price) stabilizing. But, since an increased amount of the commodity may be sold when demand rises—a rise in the " shadow " price— its supply may expand at the expense of other commodities for which it is a substitute, leading eventually to a rise in the prices of such substitutes. Only when the rigid price is the price of a factor of production, and the units excluded from sale by the rigid price are wholly unemployed, does the stabilizing influence of the rigid price outweigh the destabilizing effects on the supply side. *Ibid.*, pp. 266-269.

29 *Ibid.*, p. 269.

30 *Ibid.*, p. 269.

rational for them to fix wage-rates in money terms at a level which seems to them 'fair' in relation to this 'normal' price level...

In order to explain wages, we have to assume in the parties to the wage-bargain some sense of normal prices, hardly distinguished (perhaps) from 'just' prices...

There must be a tendency to rigidity of certain prices, particularly wage-rates; but there must also be a tendency to rigidity of certain price-expectations as well, in order to provide an explanation for the rigidity of these prices.[31]

Hicks' case for rigid wage-rates, and for what stability there is, rests merely on the inference that there is some " sense of normal prices " in the parties to the wage-bargain. Beyond asserting that sensitivity of price expectations depends " on the psychological condition of the individuals trading ", he gives no satisfactory account of how expectations of different elasticity —especially the critical case of inelastic expectations which make for rigid wage-rates—are formed on the basis of price experience alone.[32] We are left only with the belief that, if we are to get a " reasonably realistic model of the economic system," price-expectations among the " individuals trading " *must* have a tendency to rigidity.

In the absence of a causal explanation of price-expectations which would distinguish between the element of price experience in expectations and possible reactions to institutional events in general, Hicks' theory of price fluctu-

31 *Ibid.*, pp. 270-271.

32 Hicks suggests the following classification of influences which may affect price-expectations: " non-economic " influences include such factors as the weather, political news, peoples' state of health, and their psychology. Another group of influences, though still not closely connected with actual price-movements, consists of market superstitions at one extreme, and news bearing on the future movements of demand and supply at the other. " The third ", says Hicks, " consists of actual experience of prices, experience in the past and experience in the present.... For the purpose of our inquiry, changes in price-expectations which result from either of the first two sorts of influence have to be treated as autonomous changes." *Ibid.*, p. 204.

ations remains incomplete. He has limited himself rather
severely in a " work on Theoretical Economics, considered as
the logical analysis of an economic system of private enterprise,
without any inclusion of reference to institutional controls."
His method of analysis cannot be pushed beyond its confines.
The price-system is " not inherently and necessarily stable ".
But the reasons must be sought, perhaps, in forces which,
though influencing price-expectations, lie outside the framework of (short-term) equilibrium analysis.

The Concept of Expectations

An imposing amount of discussion has been devoted to the
subject of expectations (and anticipations) in recent theoretical
literature. Its gist is that expectations and anticipations represent probability estimates made by individuals (firms and consumers) with respect to the data (tastes, resources, market conditions) in forming plans to buy or sell goods at
a future date. What actually governs the adoption of a particular plan depends not on " the most probable price expected
to rule " unchanged at some future date, but on the " dispersion of possible prices ".[33] An increased dispersion makes an
individual more uncertain about expected prices and less will-
ing to make plans which involve buying or selling at a given
date. " If we are to allow for uncertainty of expectations in
these problems of the determination of plans ", Hicks adds,
" we must not take the most probable price as the representative expected price, but the most probable price plus or minus
an allowance for the uncertainty of the expectation, that is to
say, an allowance for risk." [34]

" Risk " may also be interpreted as " the dispersion of the
frequency distribution of alternative future events and ' uncertainty ' as the degree of ignorance about this frequency dis-

33 *Ibid.*, p. 125.
34 *Ibid.*, p. 126.

tribution ".[35] Professor Marschak explains the concept of uncertain expectations when he writes, " . . . the investor when visualizing the range of alternative losses or profits which may arise, is not concerned merely with some average (be it the 'expected value' . . . or some other form of average) ; he is concerned also, for example, with the dispersion of the profits, in whatever way this may be measured (the standard deviation, the difference between the highest and the lowest possible profit or some other measure) . . . Dispersion may be taken as a measure of ' risk '; its reciprocal would measure the ' safety' of an asset. The tendency to put a high estimate on the expected values of profits (or some other average) we have called ' optimism '. The tendency to estimate a low dispersion of profits—low risks—may be called ' confidence '." [36]

The notion of " confidence " is closely linked with the problem of expectations and anticipations. In Hicks' discussion of fluctuations stability of the price-system rests on " confidence in a stable value of money ", or the persistence of a " normal " level of prices.[37] " Confidence " is also an element in the calculation of risks—i. e., the " tendency to estimate a low dispersion of profits," or the spread around some average price or profit.[38] The question of " confidence " and its significance for business planning is bound up with the problem of deducing changes in anticipations from the objective data; and this " . . . needs judg-

---

35 H. Makower and J. Marschak, *op. cit.*, p. 271, f. 1. " The term *uncertainty* then refers to the fact that 'risk' exists, i. e. that no event is assigned the probability 1 (and therefore the dispersion is greater than zero) . . . we are not ignorant about the probabilities which are assigned to the various alternative events; yet there is uncertainty even there about each single event."

36 J. Marschak, " Lack of Confidence ", *Social Research*, February, 1941, p. 53.

37 Hicks, *op. cit.*, p. 270.

38 Makower and Marschak, *loc. cit.*

ment and knowledge of business psychology much more than sustained logical reasoning." [39]

If we could explain the factors that make for business confidence or for lack of confidence, we would know a great deal more about changes in business expectations and how they may bring on economic fluctuations. There are two ways in which equilibrium analysis might conceivably provide such an explanation. First, through the introduction of anticipations, a theory of fluctuations could be advanced in which " . . . all factors influencing business activity are taken to act through business men's estimates and plans." [40] In this case equilibrium analysis does not give us a complete theory of fluctuations because " the effect of the first event on anticipations cannot be rigorously determined." [41] Any number of factors may influence business confidence, may affect prices and profit margins and cause fluctuations. Second, equilibrium analysis might offer a self-contained theory in which fluctuations are inherent in the price system itself, rather than the result of factors acting on the price system from the outside. Fluctuations would then have to be explained solely in terms of changes in the variables pertinent to temporary equilibrium analysis, i. e., reactions to changes in tastes, techniques, resources and prices. For example, it is generally assumed that price-expectations are formed on the basis of the record of prices in the past and present; but that record is the result of attitudes which prevailed at an earlier period and so on in an indefinite backward sequence. If expectations were formed *only* on the basis of price-experience in the immediate past and present, fluctuations around prices believed to be " normal " might be more severely limited than they are in practice. The sole source of judgment regarding the future would then be the fact that prices had been, and were,

39 Hicks, "A Suggestion for Simplifying the Theory of Money," *loc. cit.*

40 Albert G. Hart, " Business Planning and the Cycle," *Quarterly Journal of Economics*, February, 1937, p. 296.

41 *Ibid.*, p. 279.

" normal " and that prices would continue so. If business men change their minds about prices which have been regarded as " normal," as they often do, other factors besides price-experience must have an important bearing on judgments respecting future prices when current prices change.

What are some of these factors? They may include guesses about the future course of wage-rates and labor's demands, government investment and tax policy, the plans of rival firms, central bank policy, new technique and so on. This list could undoubtedly be expanded, but it will serve as an example. Although the importance of each factor taken separately may vary considerably at different times, it is some such group of factors that we have in mind when we speak of the confidence of the business community or its psychology. Furthermore, business men (including investors) and the general public probably have different reactions to price changes and estimate the stability of money in different ways. It may be correct to say, as Hicks does, that the general public bases its estimates of the stability of a currency almost entirely on the past and present record of prices. But any business man prides himself on his ability to gauge other factors besides the past record of prices in deciding whether to move ahead confidently, or cautiously or to retrench.[42] Whether businessmen are successful in forming even rough probability estimates of the future is another matter. Professor Mitchell seems to sum up the contrary view when he observes,

42 As evidence of the importance of this distinction a banker of the author's acquaintance has noted that businessmen, in contrast to the general public, attempted to include other factors beside past and current prices in forming their judgments, even in pre-World War I days when prices and currencies were relatively stable. The distinction between the public and businessmen on this score was certainly less sharp after World War I. People are notoriously affected by the political climate, by confidence or lack of confidence in a government, by the fear of sharp social change, etc., circumstances which played an important part in German hyperinflation during the twenties and are currently (autumn of 1948) producing a financial crisis in France.

... profits depend on two variables—margins between selling and buying prices and on the volume of trade—related to each other in unstable fashion, and subject to perturbations from a multitude of unpredictable causes. That the system of prices has its own order is clear; but it is not less clear that this order fails to afford certainty of business success. Men of long experience and proved sagacity often find their calculations upset by conjunctures which they could not anticipate. Thus the money economy confuses the guidance of economic activity by interjecting a large element of chance into every business venture.[43]

In making uncertain expectations the central problem in their analysis, the theorists who employ (temporary) equilibrium analysis have touched on an important source of instability in a system of private enterprise without explaining fluctuations. They have suggested factors that influence businessmen and the public in forming judgments to sell and buy goods and in adjusting their plans in the face of uncertainty. Business men try to judge the uncertain future by using the information at hand—past and current profits and prices and the factors which may affect these quantities. From the vantage of the individual businessman many of these factors are the result of chance. rather than past experience, and he frequently has little or no basis for forming judgments about them. For the economy as a whole, individual adjustments to uncertainty and " chance " may produce instability and lead to cumulative movements of contraction or expansion.

The factors that may influence expectations through " business confidence " and " business psychology " seem, on the whole, to lie outside the scheme of equilibrium analysis. The totality of economic and non-economic factors comprising business confidence would logically be supposed to register on the price-system studied in equilibrium analysis. For certain pur-

---

43 Wesley C. Mitchell, *Business Cycles* (Berkeley: University of California Press, 1913), p. 39.

poses economic analysis may be held to this type of inquiry. But in an inquiry concerned with the causes of business fluctuations it may not be enough to examine the end-result of shifts in business confidence, as they may register on the price-system. The forces responsible for changes in business confidence— economic and non-economic — call for independent analysis when they are brought in as the main cause of fluctuations.

Theoretical economists in the past have shied away from questions which could not be fitted into a determinate analysis. By determinate we mean the type of uniformities studied in equilibrium analysis, namely the tendency toward equality of supply and demand at a particular set of prices. Yet many of the problems bound up with economic fluctuations seem to be of the indeterminate variety. " The problem is ' indeterminate ', writes Joan Robinson, " when the specifically economic factors (that is, factors the economist has been accustomed to handle), do not serve to provide a unique solution, so that ' non-economic ' factors have to be brought into the story before an answer to the problem can be found. ' Non-economic ' factors, such as human error or sentimentality, political disturbances, the state of confidence in the currency, or the strategical position of Trade Unions, are those which cannot easily be fitted into the existing structure of pure economic analysis." [44] These are the kinds of questions we seem to evade when we attempt to force the problem of economic fluctuations into the mold of equilibrium analysis.

To summarize, the type of theory which has been developed around the concept of temporary equilibrium does not explain the forces which actually govern fluctuations. What this theory does explain is how hypothetical adjustments to changing prices may (possibly) bring on cumulative upward or downward price movements. If price expectations are inelastic, substitution between money and goods can restore equilibrium when prices

[44] Joan Robinson, *Essays in The Theory of Employment,* (2nd ed., New York: Macmillan, 1948), p. 171.

change (rise or fall). But this necessary condition, or its absence, cannot be deduced from the price-system under analysis —the system of prices, and the conditions determining prices, given by the equations of general equilibrium theory. Changes in expectations and stability or instability are governed by factors lying partly, or even mainly, outside this system of explanation. The attempt to explain expectations as probability estimates has resulted in considerable refinement of such concepts as " risk " and " uncertainty." The causation of expectations in rigorous theoretical terms, however, has not been established.

The role of money is discussed extensively in temporary equilibrium analysis; but the action of money is limited in the short-run to substitution relations between goods, money, and securities. " Money " as an instrument of capital investment, the relation between capital investment and consumption, the factors which may deter or promote investment, the effects of these relations on income and employment—these aspects of the problem of fluctuations are in part abstracted in " expectations " and the substitution relations, or passed over entirely because they fall outside the scope of temporary equilibrium analysis. Above all, a method of analysis viewed as " pure theory ", a method which seeks the generality of mathematical logic, can hardly be expected to give us a theory which explains the business fluctuations of reality.

CHAPTER IV
THE INFLUENCE OF SWEDISH SEQUENCE ANALYSIS

THE work of the Swedish economists occupies a unique position in contemporary economic thought. Keynes' theory of employment, Hicks' theory of temporary equilibrium, and econometric analysis all owe much to original contributions by Swedish economists. Though the debt has been acknowledged,[1] Swedish theory constitutes far more than a transitional body of economic thought. For it is the Swedish economists who were the first among contemporary theorists to investigate systematically the problem of changes in the general price level, changes that may lead to cumulative contraction or expansion of the economic system.

In Swedish theory the analysis of changing expectations and anticipations, of planning periods, and of the relation between saving, investment, and consumption, have been developed around the problem of how changes in the general price level originate and run their course. These are among the principal problems with which contemporary Anglo-Saxon theory is also concerned. But there is an important difference between the sort of theory developed by the Swedish School[2] and that advanced by Hicks and by the Keynesian and econometric theorists. Swedish analysis is not an equilibrium analysis. In Swedish theory economic plans and decisions are supposed to be formed on the basis of anticipations and expectations that are not mutually compatible, that involve inequality (say) of saving and investment for the economy at large. Moreover, expectations and anticipations are continually revised in the light of

1 *Cf.* A. P. Lerner, "Some Swedish Stepping Stones in Economic Theory", *Canadian Journal of Economics and Political Science*, VII, 1941, pp. 559-562. J. Tinbergen, *op. cit.*, I, 13-14. J. R. Hicks, *op. cit.*, p. 3.

2 *Cf.* Ohlin, "The Stockholm Theory of Savings and Investment", *op. cit.*, p. 92.

realized results and new estimates of the future so that changing plans bring changes in saving, investment and consumption, which bring changes in realized results (e. g., profits), which induce revision of expectations and anticipations, and so on in an indefinite sequence of actions and reactions. In terms of this theoretical outlook the system need not come to rest at any particular level of economic activity. In Swedish process analysis we have a body of theory which is closely related to the several theories discussed in this study but, unlike the other theories, one from which the implications of an equilibrium tendency are absent.

Many economists have contributed to the development of Swedish theory. It is therefore not always possible under the circumstances to discuss Swedish theory in terms of contributions made by individual economists of the Swedish group.[3]

The Theory of the Cumulative Process

Wicksell's discussion of the cumulative process underlies the whole brilliant achievement of contemporary Swedish economists. Wicksell gives us an early statement of the causal connections between saving, consumption and investment and of their order of movement in economic expansion and contraction. The idea of the cumulative process is basically dynamic and represents a decisive break with general equilibrium analysis and the theory of relative prices. But the theory of the cumulative process underwent much refinement and even restatement before it emerged in its present-day form.

Wicksell attempted to explain cumulative movements of the whole economy in terms of divergence between (aggregate) savings and investment: for example, total demand will rise under given conditions of supply when people purchase capital goods (and inventory) for sums in excess of available (current)

---

3 The following discussion is based on Swedish sources of prewar vintage, frequently dating back to the period of the great depression. Views have naturally changed over the years. But the main implications of Swedish process analysis for dynamic theory are not likely to have been altered.

savings. Increased investment means increased income possibilities, including higher prices and profits. Once started the process of expansion is not likely to come to a stop, but keeps going in self-accelerating fashion. The causal explanation of the expansion (or contraction) depends on a fundamental relation between the money (i. e., " normal ") rate of interest, determined by credit conditions, and the real (i. e., " natural ") rate, viewed as the (marginal) physical productivity of capital. The interest rate plays a fundamental role because it determines the price relation between capital goods and consumption goods. When the money rate declines, or when the " natural " rate of interest rises, say, because of improved technique, and the money rate does not follow suit, the value of existing (real) capital rises. The production of capital goods then becomes relatively more profitable than production of consumption goods. Entrepreneurs draw away factors of production from the consumption goods industries by bidding higher prices on the basis of improved profit opportunities in the production of capital goods. But the prices of consumption goods tend to rise too, in part because the supply is reduced when the production of capital goods is favored, and in part because demand for consumption goods rises as increased capital investment results in a higher national income. Since capital values are partly determined by anticipated prices of consumption goods, rising prices in the consumption goods industries stimulate further capital investment. The expansion continues so long as the " natural " rate of interest exceeds the money rate. In Wicksell's discussion the expansion is halted when the banking system takes steps to increase the money rate of interest in relation to the " natural " rate, thus starting a cumulative process in the opposite (downward) direction. Wicksell's theory of the cumulative process therefore is not a self-contained theory of the business cycle: the process starts and is reversed when factors outside the system of explanation—credit or technological conditions—are altered.[4]

4 In his lectures Wicksell attempted to explain how credit and technical changes enter directly into the cumulative process. See Knut Wicksell,

The important element in the cumulative process is the expected increase in profits and incomes generally when the real (natural) rate of interest for one reason or another comes to exceed the money rate. When the money rate of interest declines, or the natural rate rises while the money rate lags behind, the relative decrease in the rate of discount raises price and profit expectations. The proximate cause of a monetary expansion is increased investment in capital goods industries in the expectation that prices and profits will rise. The saving required for an expansion of capital investment then will be forthcoming as a result of higher anticipated business profits. For, with rising prices, a shift in the income distribution takes place in favor of entrepreneurs sufficient to increase total savings in an amount equal to new investment.[5] The expansion continues because total purchasing power rises when investment is increased; and the increased demand for consumption goods leads to further expectation of price and profit increases and to additional capital investment. However, the role of expectations and anticipations in an expansion—especially the causal connection between higher anticipated profits from investment and increased savings needed to finance an expansion — was not brought out clearly by Wicksell. He suggests that price and profit-expectations change when the money and natural rates of interest diverge; and there is a similar, implicit assumption about further stages of the cumulative process, as income expectations rise and lead to increased consumption expenditure. But the sequence of reactions that determines the expansion is not stated precisely. At the hands of Wicksell's followers ex-

---

Lectures on Political Economy (London: Routledge, 1935), II, 5-6. But as Lundberg points out, causal connections are not worked out as carefully in the Lectures as in Wicksell's other work.

5 The manner in which increased capital investment is financed—i. e. through a shift to profits—as well as the exact relation between investment and consumption goods during an expansion was worked out by Lindahl in terms of Wicksell's basic concepts. For a discussion of the shift to profits during an expansion see Erik Lindahl, *Studies in the Theory of Money and Capital* (New York: Farrar, 1940), pp. 173-176.

pectations and anticipations were brought into the theory of the cumulative process as the determining (and determined) factors in an expansion (or contraction) of economic activity.

Wicksell's concept of the real ("natural") rate of interest furnishes an especially good example of the direction taken by this restatement of the theory of cumulative process. Lindahl, Myrdal, and later Lundberg pointed out that Wicksell took the real rate of interest—i. e., the expected yield on investment—as given and that he merely assumed the real rate would remain unchanged during a given period of production. But changes in the expected yield on capital investment play an important, and even crucial, part in the cumulative process. In setting themselves the task of bringing such factors as the real rate of interest into their analysis, the Swedish economists introduced a number of innovations which eventually paved the way for a distinctive theory of economic dynamics.

For example, one of the central problems in the cumulative process is to explain how deviations between the money rate of interest and the real rate give rise to more (or less) favorable profit expectations. In tackling this problem,[6] Myrdal developed his celebrated distinction between ex post and ex ante periods, a distinction which is fundamental to Swedish sequence analysis. The notion of ex ante and ex post led logically to that of planning periods and to the idea of a coordinated sequence of reactions in which plans extending into the future are determined by experience (of prices, profits, income, savings, etc.) in a preceding period. A precise period analysis meant that the theory of the cumulative process could be put into far more exact form. With this distinction in mind it is possible, for example, to see how an expansion takes place when planned savings and planned investment are unequal (ex ante). Investment ex ante will exceed savings ex ante because of divergent anticipations of different economic groups in the community—

6. Gunnar Myrdal, *Monetary Equilibrium* (London: Hodge, 1939), pp. 51-57, 65.

entrepreneurs, persons with contractual earnings, investors, workers, etc. When entrepreneurs increase investment at the beginning of a period even though planned savings fall short of planned investment, the result is a price expansion in which entrepreneurs realize profits sufficiently large to make total savings at the end of the period correspond to the value of real investment achieved during the period. Realized investment (ex post) and realized savings (ex post) will be found to be equal. The notion of ex post and ex ante periods explains in precise terms how increased investment is financed when the money rate of interest declines.

The possibility of including changes in the real and money rates of interest in a sequence analysis of the cycle has been explored most recently by Erik Lundberg. Lundberg develops several different models of an expansion and of possible turning points. In one of his models the expansion is explained in terms of the acceleration principle.[7] The expansion is supposed to take place over a series of periods in relation to " rational responses " to changes studied in the analysis. For example, investments are directly correlated with consumer outlay on the assumption that there is a given fixed relation between the increase in demand for consumption goods and new investment. Increased

---

[7] Lundberg observes that some of his models "... agree especially well with the main features of Clark's picture of the business cycle " (as presented in Strategic Factors in Business Cycles) ; and that the models "... may be regarded as an attempt to give precision to some of his (Clark's) arguments, by setting them in relation to a determinate system." Erik Lundberg, Studies in the Theory of Economic Expansion (New York: King, 1937), p. 253. Lundberg's analysis at other points is reminiscent of Harrod's notion of a " warranted " rate of expansion, Kalecki's analysis of the effect of continued investment activity on the total quantity of and demand for capital, and more recent studies by Domar of the rate of investment required to maintain an expansion. See Chapters V and VI of this study. In fact Lundberg makes a point that has only recently been considered in Keynesian literature: that the marginal efficiency of capital cannot be regarded as given without reference to a certain rate of expansion, an expansion which must be explained in a truly dynamic theory. Lundberg, op. cit., p. 180.

investment [8] generates an increase in total income and the inducement to continue increasing production by introducing new capital units depends on the expansion of industrial markets (effective demand). At the same time the increase in total income and effective demand depend on continued new investment. But new investment cannot keep rising at a rate sufficient to maintain an increase in expected receipts [9] which must cover costs, i. e., operations, maintenance, amortization, and interest and profits. There is a growing disparity between savings and investment as " non-income generating costs ", for example, amortization charges, rise during an expansion. As the rate of new investment falls, income and effective demand fall off and the expansion is reversed.

The second type of expansion considered by Lundberg depends on long-term investments, e. g., railroads, shipbuilding, new housing, etc. Here the long-term rate of interest is the determining factor in the expansion. The long-term rate rises during an expansion and leads to an increasing discrepancy between savings and investment so that the growing insufficiency of (gross) savings results in the breakdown of long-term investments. Lundberg suggests that the effect of the two types of investments on an expansion will depend on the investment goods involved. Conditions on the capital market will have more weight in determining the volume of activity—than direct demand for consumer goods—when long-term investments predominate. " The degree of dependence of investments upon the direct demand for consumption goods ", says Lundberg, " may be supposed to decrease with the length of the period of construction and the durability of the capital goods in question." [10] Lundberg suggests too that, under conditions where long-term

8 Profits are supposed to have increased (say) because of a fall in the money rate of interest.

9 The real rate of interest is analogous to the marginal efficiency of capital, i. e., income is generated in relation to the expected future yield of new investment planned by entrepreneurs. *Cf.* Lundberg, *op. cit.*, p. 176.

10 *Ibid.*, p. 254.

investments predominate in an expansion, a breakdown of long-term investment—as the rate of interest rises—may bring a reversal of the expansion apart from any initial failure of demand for consumption goods. That is, when long-term investments are reduced, the decline in income and demand may curtail investment dependent on the growth of consumer demand and lead to a reversal of the expansion.

THE UNIT-PERIOD

Swedish sequence analysis represents a theoretical apparatus that departs completely from traditional equilibrium notions. The analysis is concerned with plans made by entrepreneurs and income recipients with respect to production, consumption, investment, and savings. Plans, formed on the basis of past (realized) results, are not compatible, e. g., planned investment and savings, income, and expenditure, etc. are not equal. Since individual plans and decisions vary, changes in investment, production, income and saving will result when plans are carried out during a period. These changes will affect the income position of different groups, say, a transfer of income from fixed-income recipients to entrepreneurs, or from the producers of consumption goods to the producers of capital goods. The changes in investment, production, consumption and saving are such that the realized values of receipts, investment, savings, etc. are generally different from the expected values. Reactions to these changes set the stage for subsequent plans with respect to production, consumption, saving and investment. In short, we have a time sequence, a succession of events.

Swedish analysis attempts to provide a determinate theory of economic expansion and, at the same time, one that is not confined to a fixed scheme of variables and constants. The sequence of events is explained in terms of factors contained in the system of explanation, namely realized results flowing from preceding plans and reactions to such results. There is, however, no suggestion that the system tends toward a particular level of economic activity. Rather, the sequence of plans and reactions to changes wrought by plans results in cumulative movement of prices and national income. " The sequence of changes ", writes Lundberg, " will continuously upset the given conditions to which adjustments are supposed to take place." [11] Swedish sequence analysis studies (monetary) disequilibria which lead to a succession of plans and economic decisions, of realized results, of reactions to realized results, of further plans, etc. The " data " of traditional theory become variables to be explained by the analysis.

There are several methodological problems. First, a determinate analysis should indicate what weight should be attached to different reactions to realized results. Second, such an analysis should indicate how and with what time lags reactions to realized results affect different determining factors, namely the effect on investment, savings, consumption, etc. Third, since sequence analysis deals with changes in investment, saving, and consumption in the economy at large, there must be some provision for the summation of plans made by individual entrepreneurs and income recipients and for their combined reactions to change.

In Swedish analysis an attempt is made to meet these problems through the concept of the unit-period, a time interval which depends on the problem at hand. If, for example, the period considered is of too brief duration, there will not be a sufficient time lag between changes in profits, sales and prices on the one hand and reactions by producers and consumers on the other. Actually individuals do not react immediately to very small changes by altering their plans in terms of the scale of production, prices, consumption, savings, etc. The concept of the unit-period depends on the assumption that,

> The changes may accumulate during a certain time before the individual decides to alter his plans. The length of time will depend upon a number of circumstances, such as the size of the initial changes, periods of contract, production period, etc. The new operations arising during an infinitesimal time-

11 Lundberg, *op. cit.*, p. 246.

element will therefore necessarily refer to a very small group of individuals, and the explanation of their reaction and its consequences will have the character of a partial analysis. ... the development of the whole economy cannot very well be explained by summing up the results of partial theories.[12]

In other words, since the analysis seeks to explain changes in the economy at large, the interval of time selected as the unit-period must be long enough for changes to affect all individuals in the economy. On the other hand, the unit-period selected may be too long for a particular type of analysis, i. e., changes may occur within the period which cannot be accounted for in the analysis.[13]

The unit-period defines the time lag between the realized values of investment, saving, receipts, etc.—in relation to expected values—and reactions to realized results, thus giving the " speeds of reaction " which determine how quickly new plans are made. Since changes accumulate for a certain time before plans are changed, the magnitude of reactions is also defined by the length of the unit-period. Here it becomes necessary, however, to examine the reactions of different groups in the economy. The broad division of groups into producers and consumers is not sufficient. Rather, these groups have to be further subdivided to determine responses to realized results within different groups. " No limit may be set ", says Lundberg, " to our predilection for dividing groups into sub-groups on the basis of differences of reaction. These differences depend on all kinds of circumstances, from those dealing with the special character of individual enterprise under special conditions to the general character of whole groups in industry

12 *Ibid.*, p. 47.

13 As might be the case (say) in tracing changes in investment where the unit-period is based on long-run construction. Producers of consumption goods may react more quickly to realized profits or losses and change their plans unexpectedly within the period. Here the unit-period would have to be shortened to the production period required to turn out consumption goods. See Lundberg, *ibid.*, pp. 49-50.

and trade." [14] The difficulty of course is that endless subdivision into groups increases the number of possible reactions to a point where there are too many variables to be studied and the analysis becomes too cumbersome.

There are other problems connected with the concept of the unit-period. For example, the unit-period and the time lags of reactions to realized results actually vary considerably for individual producers and consumers. The unit-period is simply a device for averaging reactions of a group of similar individuals (producers or consumers) and can be made more realistic by subdividing groups, say, entrepreneurs, into component groups and choosing (shorter) unit-periods appropriate to the reaction patterns of the sub-groups.[15] Even then the concept of the unit-period rests on a critical assumption about the average behavior of different individuals within a group: that the patterns of reaction defined in terms of the unit-period persist throughout an expansion. And when the subdivision of economic groups is carried too far, we have in Lundberg's words, only a partial analysis which cannot explain changes in the economy at large.

The question is whether the sequence of changes studied in Swedish sequence analysis is really determinate, whether the chain of events can be rigorously traced back to plans and actions arising out of past results studied in the analysis. This and related methodological problems are carefully examined by Lundberg in constructing model sequences of an expansion. Lundberg is aware of the schematic nature of his models and of the restrictive character of his assumptions. Reaction patterns of producers and consumers will be constant over a period of time only by accident. Reactions by individuals to " . . . changing economic conditions will spread over an indefinite period,

14 *Ibid.*, p. 172.

15 For example, producers may be subdivided into producers of investment and consumption goods and further subdivided within this classification according to size of firm, degree of competition, type of product, amount of fixed costs, period of production, etc.

making the assumption of simultaneous changes in operations at discontinuous points in time unreal." [16] Moreover, since the rational responses, say, of producers, are based on the relation between expectations and realized results during a past period, the concept of " rational responses " may hold only " . . . to a very limited extent." [17]

Lundberg introduces a number of other qualifications that indicate the need for avoiding mechanical relations and over-simplification in sequence analysis.[18] His distinction between (1) long-term investments which are dependent primarily on changes in the capital market—namely on savings determined by the long-term rate of interest—and (2) investments dependent on the current demand for consumption goods is a case in point.[19] The greater realism in the analysis of an expansion made possible by this distinction introduces certain problems. Long-term investments—e. g., the construction of railroads and ships—may depend more on expectations as to long-term interest rates and less on the current level of consumer demand. Yet Lundberg makes the increase in long-term investment—through an increase in the expected rate of return—dependent entirely on an increase in savings and a lowered long-term interest rate. In fact, the turning point in an expansion may come when the supply of gross savings in relation to the demand for new long-run investments is " ' insufficient ' ". That is, a rise in the long-term interest rate during an expansion reduces long-run investments, lowers effective demand and causes a break in the expansion. Lundberg's analysis of an expansion may be determinate in respect to the effect on long-run investments of changes in the (long-term) rate of interest; but at the same time it simplifies and, as he himself observes, omits other relevant causal factors. When long-term investment enters in the

16 *Ibid.*, p. 243.

17 *Loc. cit.*

18 *Ibid.*, p. 244.

19 *Ibid.*, Chapter IX and pp. 253-255.

explanation of an expansion—as it must in a realistic analysis —it becomes difficult indeed to link expectations closely to past economic results. Nonetheless, it is difficult to take issue with the restrained view that " However sceptical one may be about assumed, definite relations, it is also evident that expectations about investments as well as the actual volume of investments are far from independent of current and past experience as to profits and prices. To place the volume of investments in an ordered system of relations means, then, an attempt to isolate and stress the rational elements that are present in every instance, although to an unknown and changing extent." [20]

A Note on Methodology

Temporary equilibrium analysis, Keynesian theory, and econometric analysis have much in common with Swedish theory. These methods of analysis deal with reactions to changing data and the effects of such reactions on prices (Hicks), the development of a system of relations from an initial position (econometric theorists), and relations between saving, investment, and employment given by the marginal efficiency of capital, the rate of interest and the propensity to consume (Keynesian theory). Unlike Swedish sequence analysis, however, these theories assume that the economic system tends to reach, or move toward, an equilibrium level of employment or prices. There are reactions and adjustments to changing data, but these adjustments do not alter the data which change independently. When the economic system is disturbed and an equilibrium position is disrupted, automatic adjustments occur which tend to restore price (Hicks) or employment-equilibrium (Keynes). On the other hand, the analysis employed by the Swedish economists abandons this assumption by incorporating changes in the " data " in the system of explanation. Thus changes in the quantity of capital, in the rate of interest, in consumption, and in the volume of investment are explained in terms of determinate reactions on the part of different groups in the economy to a

20 *Ibid.*, p. 176.

sequence of realized results, altering from period to period. The system does not settle down to or tend toward a particular (equilibrium) level of economic activity, but moves upward or downward as the case may be. While the other theories considered in this study owe much to Swedish analysis, they differ quite fundamentally from Swedish theory in their concentration on a closed (equilibrium) scheme. While the reasons for this divergence may seem to be purely methodological, the methodological differences reflect basic differences in the analysis of cyclical (or other) fluctuations and in the realism of the respective theories.

Besides their fundamental contribution to the theory of cumulative process, the Swedish economists have laid the basis for an accurate theoretical statement of the dynamic problem. Lindahl suggested long ago that " ... the systematic exposition of economic theory should begin with general dynamic structures and then proceed to more particular (i. e., static) assumptions ... ".[21] And he suggests even more succinctly that " ... we may conclude that static theory represents a special application of general dynamic theory for stationary conditions. " [22] The relation between dynamic and static theory has recently received considerable attention in the literature in connection with the restatement of the stability conditions of equilibrium by Professors Samuelson and Lange. Lindahl's formulation of the relation between statics and dynamics was not intended to meet this type of problem. But the concepts and relations developed in Swedish analysis have an important, though perhaps indirect, bearing on recent refinements of the concept of stability of equilibrium and afford a commentary on its relevance in economic analysis. The problem is important because the stability conditions are supposed to explain how reactions take place to restore an equilibrium when it is disturbed.

Hicks in *Value and Capital* uses the concept of stability of equilibrium in considering changes in a temporary equilibrium.

21 Lindahl, *op. cit.*, p. 34.

22 *Ibid.*, p. 32. See also p. 33.

In brief, the system changes from one period to the next (the " week ") as the data change and anticipations and plans are revised. Plans are also subject to change when price-expectations are revised. In fact, changing price-expectations may lead to cumulative contraction or expansion of the (price) system if expectations are elastic, i. e., if future prices are expected to continue rising when current prices rise.

Thus far we have a certain similarity to Swedish process analysis. But the similarity breaks down on at least two counts. First, the Swedish economists do not attach much significance to equilibrium explanations.[23] On the whole it is their view that, if an equilibrium is assumed to be temporary during a given period of time, the expectations and anticipations of different individuals, on the basis of which plans were formed, must have been incompatible. The whole notion of cumulative movement in Swedish theory rests in fact on the mutual incompatibility of plans resulting from varying anticipations and expectations held by different individuals.[24] Only when a period has ended (i. e., in retrospect) is an (accounting) balance struck (say) between total investment and total saving. Second, the Swedish economists are critical of the equilibrium concept because in Swedish analysis the revision of expectations and anticipations is not confined to price-expectations alone but covers a far broader area of analysis. Thus the analysis includes expectations of income as well as planned saving, investment, and consumption. For example, equality of planned saving and investment need not signify monetary equilibrium because even then income expectations may rise and cause cumulative expansion. Above

___

23 Although Myrdal's position on this score is not entirely clear, he does point out that the notion of monetary equilibrium is not comparable to that of general equilibrium in the traditional sense. *Cf.* Myrdal, *op. cit.*, pp. 34-37. " Monetary equilibrium " is a purely conceptual affair—a hypothetical " norm "—for judging how inequality of the natural and real rates of interest may lead to cumulative movements. Ohlin and Lundberg do not use the concept. Lundberg speaks of the " requirements of a ' dynamic equilibrium ' ", meaning the hypothetical rate of new investment needed to maintain full use of capacity. *Cf.* Lundberg, *op. cit.*, pp. 240, 254.

24 For example see Lindahl, *op. cit.*, p. 69.

all, Swedish analysis takes note of different " speeds of reaction ", in relation to the results of successive economic plans.
The importance of this factor will be evident presently.

Now Hicks views the stability conditions of equilibrium in
the following light. An equilibrium position is stable if, when
prices rise above the equilibrium price, adjustments take place
which cause supply to exceed demand, or, when prices fall, cause
demand to exceed supply. The stability conditions explain how
equilibrium is restored when prices change. Under dynamic
conditions, i. e., when expectations are uncertain, an equilibrium
will be stable if, when the price of commodity X rises (falls),
the rise (fall) in price induces an excess (lesser) supply of X
" . . . however many (or however few) repercussions through
other markets we allow for." [25]

Hicks' application of the stability concept has been criticized
on the grounds that his criteria of stability are really static,
that he applies the stability conditions for a single-commodity
market to conditions of exchange prevailing in multiple markets.
In stating this criticism, Professor Samuelson [26] and others [27]
have noted that it cannot be assumed that, when the price of
a commodity in a given market departs from equilibrium, the
prices of commodities in all other markets are either unchanged
or instantaneously adjusted to their new equilibrium. Provision
must be made in the analysis for lag relations and for differing
speeds of reaction in different markets in response to price
changes in a single market. That is, the stability conditions of
equilibrium have to be determined from the properties of the
" corresponding " dynamic system.[28] In drawing these conclusions, Samuelson refers to the dynamic models developed by
the econometric theorists in which lags and speeds of reaction

25 Hicks, op. cit., p. 254.

26 Paul A. Samuelson, " The Stability of Equilibrium: Comparative
Statics and Dynamics ", Econometrica, April, 1941, pp. 97-120.

27 Oskar Lange, Price Flexibility and Employment, pp. 94-97. Lloyd A.
Metzler, " Stability of Multiple Markets: The Hicks Conditions ", Econometrica, October, 1945, pp. 279, 291.

28 Paul A. Samuelson, loc. cit.

are treated explicitly. "The meaning of a stable equilibrium", writes Samuelson, "presupposes a theory of dynamics, namely a theory which determines the behavior through time of all the variables from initial conditions." [29] The problem of time-lags in reactions is studied in econometric analysis in terms of a sequence analysis, yet one that differs quite radically from Swedish sequence analysis.

First, in econometric analysis the notion of ex post and ex ante periods is replaced by the more abstract conception of relations between variables at different points in time, relations which determine a movement of the variables through time from initial conditions. Instead of a psychological link between the past and present in the form of anticipations and expectations which result in certain definite reaction patterns, we find statements of "direct relationship between observable phenomena at different points in time." [30] Secondly, we find that, with the abandonment of the Swedish concept of ex ante and ex post periods, sequence analysis in the econometric version branches off into a type of analysis that has much in common with traditional equilibrium analysis and is somewhat similarly restricted in its treatment of dynamic problems. The notion of stability of equilibrium could not be developed directly from Swedish sequence analysis, from an analysis concerned with processes that do not come to rest at a particular level of economic activity. The concept of stability of equilibrium required a different, modified version of Swedish analysis for its theoretical justification; and this has been supplied by the econometric interpretation of sequence analysis.

29 *Ibid.*, p. 100. Samuelson refers to Frisch's statement of the relation between a dynamic system and the derived conditions of stable equilibrium. *Cf.* Ragnar Frisch, "On the Notion of Equilibrium and Disequilibrium", *Review of Economic Studies*, February, 1936, pp. 100, *et seq.*

30 Gottfried Haberler, *Prosperity and Depression* (3rd ed., New York: Columbia University Press, 1941), p. 253, f1.

CONCLUSION

In Swedish sequence analysis we have a highly realistic method for tracing changes that lead to expansion or contraction of the economic system. It is not a full-fledged theory of the business cycle. But it does supply certain reasonable links between different stages of a cumulative process and it suggests factors that may govern turning points.

Swedish analysis also suggests why the determination of expectations and anticipations cannot be explained in a general equilibrium analysis, say, of the type used by Hicks. The Swedish economists start with the problem of demand and supply for all goods in the economy and develop this problem in terms of relations between consumption and investment goods, relations that keep changing over successive periods of time. At least this is how Wicksell's discussion of inequality between the real and natural rates of interest has been interpreted by his followers. On the other hand, Hicks seems to have been unable to develop a truly dynamic analysis—one in which speeds of reaction and time-lags are included—because he was working with a theory of relative price-formation Here we need to make some simplified but rather unrealistic assumptions to determine how changes in the price of a single commodity may affect the prices of commodities in all other markets. When we make use of the idea of different time lags and speeds of reaction in different markets and apply that notion to the general equilibrium system, we no longer have a simple formal theory of general (price) interdependence but a highly involved set of empirical relations. These relations cannot be adapted to general equilibrium analysis without destroying its logical foundation. That is, when we introduce time lags and speeds of reaction into our analysis, we add relations that cannot be adequately explained within the limited framework of equilibrium analysis. A theory of relative price formation cannot be converted into a theory of changes in the general price level because it cannot explain—unless it assumes instantaneous adjustments in all markets—how reactions in one part of the economy may affect the remainder of the economy. In a word, Swedish sequence analysis suggests why general equilibrium analysis, as it is used (say) by Hicks, is unable to tell us how expectations and anticipations are determined.

The influence of Keynesian theory on contemporary economic thought, at least in Britain and America, has been so great that the work of the Swedish economists has sometimes been eclipsed. The Keynesian relations between the marginal efficiency of capital, the rate of interest, and the propensity to consume have their counterparts in Swedish theory. For example, the relation between the money rate of interest and the real (natural) rate correspond roughly to the Keynesian relation between the rate of interest and the marginal efficiency of capital. There is no suggestion of a stable consumption function in Swedish theory [31] or of an automatic division of income as between investment, savings and consumption. Instead we find that changes in savings during an expansion may arise for several different reasons. In the case of long-run investments the long-term rate of interest rises during an expansion and causes a break in the upward movement. In an expansion where new investment is dependent primarily on the growth of consumer demand, savings will come to exceed investments because of the need to provide for an increasingly higher proportion of fixed charges. Moreover, in trying to explain how changing anticipations and expectations determine changes in the marginal efficiency of capital and the long-term rate of interest, the Swedish economists abandon the idea of equilibrium levels which is basic to Keynes' theory of employment.

The Swedish theorists have even anticipated much that may seem novel in recent Keynesian literature. The concept of the rate of new investment required to maintain effective demand

31 However, see Myrdal, *op. cit.*, pp. 167-168, who speaks of the stable consumption habits of a population and suggests that this limits a contraction.

and full use of capacity is a case in point. Lundberg explored this problem in some detail over a decade ago. It is only recently that Keynesian theorists have been asking the question: what rate of new investment will maintain an expansion; how rapidly must new investment and effective demand grow to keep capacity fully utilized?

This is not to say that Swedish theory is a finished product or that it has all the answers. Attention has been drawn to some possible drawbacks of sequence analysis. But there is one aspect of Swedish theory that overshadows all others. This is the manner in which some of the factors considered to be " data " in traditional equilibrium analysis are regarded as variables to be explained in Swedish analysis. In studying the reaction patterns of different economic groups, the Swedish economists draw on relevant aspects of the institutional background and bring them into their analysis. The action of the banking system in changing the money rate of interest provides an example. Some of the Swedish economists, especially Lundberg, have endeavored to bring such changes into the analysis of an expansion as a factor in part determined by the previous course of an expansion, and in part determining further stages of an upward movement. Central bank policy and other related fiscal policies become part of the analysis to be explained by past economic events; and bank policy in turn determines reaction patterns that govern new investment, savings, and consumption plans. New technique is introduced for reasons inherent in previous stages of an expansion and, through the reactions of producers and income recipients, conditions subsequent stages. The data of traditional equilibrium analysis become variables to be explained by the analysis.

The Swedish economists have opened up a promising field of long-run dynamic theory. But there is little in their work to suggest there may be long-run dynamic factors that influence economic development. Relations between different groups in the economy—producers, fixed income recipients, workers, etc.—are developed only within a given context of

economic expansion or contraction. Such relations are not generalized in the form of long-run institutional relations between
economic groups—determined in part (say) by particular patterns of wealth-ownership and income distribution—which may
govern economic development. On the whole Swedish sequence
analysis suggests a method for the study of different types of
business cycle expansion and contraction, rather than a
specific theory of the cycle or of economic development. By
and large the Swedish economists are eclectic in their use of
value theory and argue for certain empirically observed
(value) relations such as the desire to maximize profits, irre-
spective of the ultilitarian justification of such behavior in
traditional theory.[32] Finally, the Swedish economists recognize
the limitations of a purely formal equilibrium analysis and
they suggest certain realistic, if pragmatic, assumptions for
bringing a wide range of factors into a determinate analysis of
the business cycle.

Addendum

THE CONCEPT OF FLUCTUATIONS IN ECONOMETRIC ANALYSIS

Econometric analysis involves a specialized field of statistical
theory which is outside the scope of the present study. But econometric analysis suggests a hypothesis of economic fluctuations
which cuts across our discussion of the dynamic problem. We
introduce the subject at this point for several reasons. First,
as a type of sequence analysis econometric analysis has several
things in common with Swedish analysis and yet is sufficiently
different to constitute a separate method. In a preceding note
we referred to the manner in which the stability conditions of
(temporary) equilibrium have been developed from the econometric version of sequence analysis. Second, while it does not
provide a theory of the cycle, econometric analysis offers a
general version of the dynamic problem, one that suggests a
mechanism which maintains cyclical swings in the economic

32 Cf. Myrdal, op. cit., p. 207.

system. Third, econometric analysis has produced a method which brings out clearly what a rigidly determined causal model means and how fluctuations are to be interpreted with reference to this sort of model.

I

The resemblance between Swedish sequence analysis and econometric analysis arises from the fact that both types of analysis are expressed in terms of " non-simultaneous events ", i. e., deal " . . . with the short-term reactions of one variate upon others, but without neglecting the lapse of time between cause and effect." [33] Then too the econometricians and the Swedish economists take an " aggregative " approach: they are both concerned with the average reactions of different economic groups or groups of industries.[34] But the resemblance stops here. In Swedish analysis, the sequence of events arises from re-actions to past results embodied in the analysis, a sequence resulting in cumulative expansion or contraction of economic activity. The econometricians advance the analytical notion of a self-contained set of relations defined by certain variables to be explained, at least one of which is related to different points of time; an equal number of relations (i. e., equations); lags and constants (i. e., numerical coefficients, say, elasticities of demand) obtained by measurements on time series; and finally "non-systematic" terms or "erratic components". This scheme is considered to be determinate when the number of relations equals the number of unknowns.[35] If the " initial values " of one

33 J. Tinbergen, *Statistical Testing of Business Cycle Theories*, I, 13.

34 That is, the reaction of groups of individuals or firms measured by certain economic conditions, namely prices, costs, incomes, and so on summed or averaged for the groups in question. This is sometimes referred to as the "macro-economic" approach, i. e., an approach concerned with the economy at large. See Tinbergen, *ibid.*, p. 14; Lindahl, *op. cit.*, p. 50.

35 A complete equation expressing a dynamic relation in the econometric sense is the following where Y represents income, p price level, U' consumption level, and the v's constants, and where it is assumed that con-

or more of the variables of the problem are given, the scheme of relations is supposed to represent a progression over time, a movement which may indicate endogenous change and fluctuations.[36] Moreover, exogenous movements may result from sudden changes in the " non-systematic " terms.

This gives us of course only a schematic system of equations. But the assumptions on which models are set up in econometric analysis imply a certain classification of causal elements: those causes which are explicitly included in the model, and those causes represented by residuals which are external to the model. The distinction between endogenous and exogenous causes is inherent in the division of all possible causes of change in the variables to be explained into " systematic " and " non-systematic " parts. That is, " non-systematic " causes connect an analytical model with sources of possible external disturbance and exogenous change. However, the exact role of non-systematic causes in econometric analysis is still controversial. For example. can we consider " important inventions " or " political events which suddenly change expectations " to be " . . . non-systematic disturbances which act largely accidentally, in an

sumption outlay depends only on income and price level in the preceding time period. The total influence of so-called " non-systematic " forces is indicated by the term $R_t^{U'}$.

$$U'_t = v_1\, Y_t + v_2\, p_{t-1} + R_t^{U'}$$

See J. Tinbergen, " Econometric Business Cycle Research ", *Readings in Business Cycle Theory*, pp. 65-69.

36The above statement of the econometric method may seem to be abstract in the extreme. But there is some justification for putting the method in general terms. In fact the notion of a system of equations bound together by a logical relationship is sometimes set up as a standard of model analysis by econometricians. " There is a piece of science of considerable extent— and use, I think — " writes Tinbergen, " to be built on the basis of our system of equations even before any special economic meaning is given to the variables involved." *Ibid.*, p. 73. Econometric analysis takes various theories of the business cycle and, by fitting them into a certain analytical scheme, expresses them in quantitative (functional) form. The significance of the theories may then be checked by statistical test.

irregular way, like lottery drawings." [37] If we do consider "non-systematic " causes in this light, then economic fluctuations may be attributed both to endogenous causes, presumably " explained " by a model, and to exogenous causes or " random " influences included in the statistical residuals. Frisch in fact has advanced such a theory of the cycle, one which makes irregular disturbances the source which maintains oscillations in the economic system. In Frisch's theory movements occur, apart from endogenous periods, which indicate periods resulting from the cumulative effect of external disturbances. This suggests an hypothesis of the cycle, often referred to as the " shock " theory, which is quite different from that developed in Swedish sequence analysis where instability is traced to causes present within the economic system. [38]

Frisch first advanced the " shock " theory in an article in the Cassel essays in the early thirties. [39] Here Frisch works out a relation between the acceleration principle and the need for cash balances in which he assumes that the need for cash balances will increase during an expansion, but that the total stock of money, or money substitutes, can not be expanded in-

[37] J. Tinbergen, *Statistical Testing of Business Cycle Theories*, p. 40. " Purely accidental causes ", says Tinbergen, " ' obeying the probability laws ' will always be classified as non-systematic. The influence of certain types of policy (e. g. tax changes) may however, be classified in either group, depending on the problems to be solved ". Tinbergen, *Econometric Business Cycle Research*, p. 65.

[38] Also in Swedish analysis unit-periods are selected with reference to certain reaction patterns. The length of the period selected is determined by the type of responses being studied, e. g. one sort of time period for reactions relating to consumption goods industries and another for capital goods industries with subsidiary breakdowns within these general categories. In econometric analysis periods are selected much more mechanically, namely by taking measurements on time series data and by setting up models without much direct reference to the different reaction patterns involved.

[39] Ragnar Frisch, *Economic Essays in Honour of Gustav Cassel*, " Propagation Problems and Impulse Problems in Dynamic Economics ", pp. 171-205. It was here too that Frisch presented the first definite outlines of the econometric approach.

finitely for various reasons. As the pressure for cash balances
rises, the rate of increase of consumption will slacken. Activity
in the producer goods industries will then be curtailed, bringing on a fall in the level of income and consumption with con-
sequent economic contraction. By selecting certain values for
his constants—capital stock, lags, need for cash, etc.—Frisch
then obtains a set of equations whose solution suggests a
primary cycle of about eight years, a secondary cycle of three
and a half years, and a third cycle of some two years duration.
But he observes that, whereas his examples show oscillations
will usually be damped, observed cycles are generally not
damped.

Frisch attempts to reconcile his hypothesis about self-
generating cycles with the facts by suggesting that his model
explains only the " propagation problem ", that is changes in a
certain set of economic relations. It is necessary to include
what Frisch calls the " impulse problem " to explain why
cycles are not damped. And the " impulse problem " refers to
" erratic shocks " which constantly upset the continuous evolution of a dynamic system and introduce " into the system the
energy necessary to maintain the swings." [40] Frisch does not
tell us precisely what economic phenomena he has in mind
when he speaks of " erratic shocks ", but confines himself to
the example of a pendulum subject to disturbances and suggests
that the " accumulation of erratic influences " maintains oscillations and, by analogy, cyclical movements in the economic
system. [41]

40 *Ibid.*, p. 197. Frisch attributes the original distinction between the
" propagation and the impulse problem " to Wicksell and writes : " He
conceived more or less definitely of the economic system as being pushed
along irregularly, jerkingly—But, on the other hand, these irregular jerks
may cause more or less regular cyclical movements." *Ibid.*, p. 198.

41 Frisch observes too that Schumpeter's theory of inventions suggests
another source of the energy needed to maintain oscillations in the economic
system. *Ibid.*, p. 203. A hypothesis similar to that advanced by Frisch was
developed independently by Professor J. M. Clark in Strategic Factors in
Business Cycles. Clark does not attempt to set up a determinate analysis

The development of econometric analysis after the publication of Frisch's essay was marked by considerable controversy over statistical assumptions with Frisch, Koopmans, Tinbergen, Haavelmo, Hurwicz, Smith and others participating in the critical discussion. In the past few years the theoretical foundation of econometric analysis has been restated and substantial agreement reached among econometricians with the formulation of the theory of simultaneous random equations. This theory suggests a procedure for testing theoretical models by applying a new method of statistical inference to observations on time series.

Frisch stated the issues involved in taking measurements on time series in an early approach to the problem: [42] because of "scatter" in the determining variables in an equation of relationship, constants obtained by the method of least squares fail to measure the degree of error in all the variables. In other words, the error formulas, which ordinarily make it possible to assign a range of variation to regression coefficients in multiple correlation analysis, do not provide a suitable test of the reliability of regression coefficients (constants) obtained by measurements on time series. A corollary of this criticism of regression analysis is that, when two or more relations among economic variables are involved, fitting equations by the method of least squares leads to contradictions. Restrictions of constancy imposed on a variable in one equation are generally inconsistent with changes in that variable in other equations of the system. Frisch proposed to deal with the problem by assuming that each variable in an equation is made up of a

---

and his discussion is less abstract than Frisch's. He suggests that the cycle may be "...the resultant of the combination of random disturbances and an economic system which transmits their effects cumulatively." Random disturbances may have two effects: first, they "keep the responses of the business system from dwindling away to zero..."; second, they "induce variations in the timing and severity of the resulting cycles." J. M. Clark, *Strategic Factors in Business Cycles*, pp. 21, 62-63.

42 Ragnar Frisch, *Statistical Confluence Analysis by means of Complete Regression Systems* (Oslo: 1934).

" systematic " part and a " non-systematic " part or " erratic " component. But he did not indicate any scheme for determining errors of sampling in connection with the " erratic " component. Instead he assumed that the " erratic " component involved non-systematic disturbances consisting of many mutually independent forces each of little importance; and in the shock theory of the cycle he suggested that the cumulative effect of these disturbances, acting at short intervals, constitutes the source which maintains cyclical swings.

The theory of simultaneous random equations attempts to provide a rigorous statement of the relations which hold between a system of " true " variables and the corresponding variables in a theoretical model. The testing of a theory against the data requires a method for determining by means of some probability scheme how well a theoretical model fits the observations. In fact, " . . . to apply statistical inference to testing the hypotheses of economic theory . . . ", writes Haavelmo, " implies such a formulation of economic theories that they represent statistical hypotheses, i. e. statements . . . regarding certain probability distributions. The belief that we can make use of statistical inference without this link can only be based upon lack of precision in formulating the problems." [43]

This approach to model analysis is based on the hypothesis of statistical inference developed by Neyman and Pearson,[44] an hypothesis which defines the problem of probability esti-

[43] T. Haavelmo, " The Probability Approach in Econometrics ", *Econometrica*, Supplement, July, 1944, iv.

[44] The Neyman-Pearson hypothesis owes a good deal to R. A. Fisher's concept of " likelihood " that is the concept distinguished from that of probability which measures an order of preference or " rational belief when we are reasoning from sample to population." R. A. Fisher, " The Logic of Inference ", *Journal of the Royal Statistical Society*, Vol. 98, 1935, p. 40. Fisher remarks that " The method of likelihood is thus an observable property of an hypothesis which specifies the values of the population sampled. Neyman and Pearson have attempted to extend the definition of likelihood to apply, not to particular hypotheses, but to classes of such hypotheses." *Ibid.*, p. 41.

mates in a rather formal way. In his pioneer study on the
application of this method to economic data Haavelmo supposes
that probability estimates can be set up for time series by taking
the right definition of the problem, that " . . . we can derive new
statements from it (the probability concept) [45] by the rules of
logic." [46] Indeed, " for the purpose of testing hypotheses it is
not even necessary to assume that the sample could actually
be repeated. We make hypothetical statements before we draw
the sample, and we are only concerned with whether the sample
rejects or does not reject an a priori hypothesis." [47] These
hypothetical statements are based on the following assumptions.
First, the whole of a time series is regarded as one observation
or sample point of n variables from a joint probability law
about which inferences can be made. By using the device of
the " sample point ", it becomes possible to drop the assumption
that successive terms are independent observations from a fixed
" population ". Second, it is assumed that a test of a statistical
hypothesis involves " . . . a rule of rejection or nonrejection
of the hypothesis, on the basis of a given sample point, and that
the probability of the decision being right or wrong is then a
" random variable ".[48]

Personal judgment weighs heavily in this as in other methods
of statistical estimation. For example, the risk in restricting a
priori hypotheses about probability " laws ", which may hold
in a problem of estimation, cannot be judged in probability
terms but is a matter of general knowledge and intuition.[49]

45 Author's note.

46 Haavelmo, *op. cit.*, p. iv.

47 *Ibid.*, p. 70.

48 *Ibid.*, p. 62.

49 *Ibid.*, p. 81. It should be added that these developments in econometric
analysis have not brought forth any new views on the theory of cyclical
(or other) fluctuations. Variables in a theoretical model are viewed as
random variables once probability estimates of the random component are
included in the model. Some econometricians have suggested that it may
not be valid procedure to identify the " external " variables in a model

And as R. A. Fisher notes, " likelihood " " . . . does not in fact obey the laws of probability ".[50] It is a different and more restricted concept than probability, one in which judgment is the main guide. Indeed, the methods of statistical estimation recently developed by econometricians have a closer affinity to historical methods than might be supposed. Differences of method may be rather trivial when, as in the social sciences, personal judgment looms so large in the solution of problems.

II

In trying to give quantitative meaning to dynamic relations, the econometricians attempt to advance beyond the formal relations found in general equilibrium analysis by setting up analytical models built around observations on the data in time series. But econometric analysis rests on a method of statistical inference which contains a basic limiting assumption. In the final anlysis, mathematical models of economic relationship depend on the premise that economic data display enough stability to estimate the probability distribution of the residuals in time series.

Econometric analysis does more than this. It tells us what an uncompromising use of mathematical logic implies for the theory of economic fluctuations. In econometric analysis a model representing a determinate scheme, namely a set of

---

with chance variables. For example, Hurwicz observes that " . . . a model in only a few variables, resulting from the elimination of many variables, has 'composite' disturbances with properties of a moving average." Leonid Hurwicz, "Aspects of the Theory of Economic Fluctuations ", *Econometrica*, January, 1945. Mitchell and Burns propose a classification of cycle patterns that opens up an alternative line of investigation of "random" forces. They suggest that differences between reference and specific cycle patterns may result from the operation of substantial random influences in the specific cycle averages. In turn differences between the two patterns may depend on a random component " . . . measured roughly by the difference between the two patterns," W. C. Mitchell and A. F. Burns, *Measuring Business Cycles*, p. 505.

50 R. A. Fisher, *Statistical Methods for Research Workers* (9th ed.; London: Oliver, 1944), p. 10.

relations and an equal number of unknowns, holds for a short period.[51] Disturbances in this sort of scheme may arise only in part within the set of relations postulated in the model, leaving a substantial part of the problem to be explained by exogenous causes. One of the other main possibilities of fluctuations then is that resulting from the cumulation of chance causes. And here an important part of the problem of economic fluctuations is left to causes which remain unexplained because they are not specifically included in the model. Like other versions of the dynamic problem discussed in this study, econometric analysis suggests an hypothesis of the causation of the cycle bound up largely with forces that lie outside the system of explanation.

The purpose of these comments is to suggest caution in using functional notions and methods of testing functional relationships which have been drawn from a wholly different field of observation. A pendulum may be a helpful analogy for drawing simplified conclusions about the mechanism of disturbance in our economic system. But we cannot, or ought not to extend the analogy so far that our methods of reasoning become bound up completely with the kind of motion found in pendulums or other mechanical systems.

Probability theory has been traditionally associated with the problem of physical measurement. Probability theory tells us approximately what limits to assign to the discrepancy between hypothesis and observations. But it supplies us with a theory of " errors " on certain conditions: that we have " ... a series of values taken by some chance variables at mutually independent trials and on the assumption of an unchangeable law of distribution." [52] When we say, for example, that planetary

51 Linear relations are generally used and this frequently requires the assumption that, over small intervals, a function may be approximated by a linear one. Then too the mathematics used, i. e. the differential calculus, is bound up with the notion of small (incremental) change.

52 A. A. Tschuprow quoted by Oskar Anderson, " The Logic of Decomposition of Statistical Series," *Journal of the Royal Society*, 1927, p. 563.

laws of motion hold within a preassigned margin of error, we mean that variations in our measurements at successive observations are chance variations rather than systematic variations that might alter the laws expressed. We make this assumption because experience has shown us that observations taken at widely separated points in time and space follow this pattern of variation. We are dealing here with repetitive events, with systems that have demonstrated a high order of persistence.

When we apply probability theory to observations on economic data without qualification, we assume that economic data display tested properties analogous to those found in physical data. We know of course from the history of social and economic institutions that relationships in this field do not have the persistence of laws of physics. The process of institutional change seems to be one of cumulation and alteration of relations rather than seeming repetition of events. When we construct analytical models for short periods, institutional change becomes part of the data. Our short period models can convey the notion of change in several ways: either through adjustments of the variables to periodic changes in data, or through lagged relations between the variables, or through disturbances in the data which are transmitted to the variables by " influences " existing outside the model. In the latter case the mechanism of disturbance may lead to fluctuations through the accumulation of " influences " which are irregular or random by definition. This suggests that economic oscillations may result from a process of cumulation, but one in which we postulate in advance that the cumulating elements are unknown random forces. The application of a strict functional logic, a logic that does not tell us anything about the forces impounded in " random factors " or the data, would seem to conceal the very forces which make our system liable to instability.

We are not saying that the complexity of events rules out causal analysis in economic science. But we do suggest that the emphasis in economic theory be shifted from a point of view completely dominated by short-run concepts of causation originating in mechanics. We may be able, for example, to set up a different framework for causal analysis in economic science by considering the long-run dynamics of the system of private enterprise. Private ownership of wealth and accumulation of wealth through production for a market are the persistent long-run features of our economic system. But these basic conditions have a way of promoting self-generating changes so that the organization of the private enterprise system is altered even though its general institutional features persist. For example, we find that abolition of the Corn Laws in England represented the culmination of an historical process which provided cheap raw materials, in turn cheapened the wage bill, gave England the labor needed for her industrial expansion, and made her dependent on overseas sources of supply and investment of British capital abroad. Or we can point to the problems posed for private ownership by the growth of technique which made large-scale production in some basic industries profitable, led to concentration, and, when scale of plant and capital investment reached formidable proportions, resulted in the taking over of control by financial and banking interests. In a word we find historical processes under way that indicate economic institutions have been changing in the past, not mechanically repeating themselves. If the dynamics of the system of private enterprise are interpreted in the light of an historical process, not a mechanical process, then we may perhaps be able to make inferences about causal forces now placed in the category of data or disturbances or random forces. If we can approach causal analysis in this way, the originating causes of cyclical (or other) fluctuations are not likely to be regarded as irregular disturbances, as chance events acting on a self-contained economic system. Instead the cycle and its causation might come to be regarded as an integral part of the economic system and its long-run development.

CHAPTER V

DYNAMIC FACTORS IN KEYNESIAN THEORY

Not much that is new can be said about the fundamentals of Keynes' theory of employment. For over a decade economists have been preoccupied with the concepts and relations set forth in the General Theory of Employment, Interest and Money. The historic role of Keynes' theory as an explanation of underemployment equilibrium in a private enterprise economy is generally accepted. The basic analysis—the schedule relations between the marginal efficiency of capital, the rate of interest and the propensity to consume which, together with the given quantity of money and given expectations, determine the (equilibrium) level of employment—has been subjected to searching study and comment. This, if anything, has strengthened its grip on contemporary economic thought. But the implications of this work are still highly controversial and offer economists many fertile possibilities. It is something of a paradox, for instance, that a substantial part of contemporary business cycle research and theory has received much of its inspiration from a theory which is supposed to be static. The key to the paradox lies in the dynamic factors suggested in the static theory, factors which provide the background for Keynes' analysis and are often woven into the static structure. It is the dynamic implications of Keynes' work with which we are principally concerned.

Perhaps the most striking feature of the Keynesian theory of employment is the manner in which the central problem of economics is shifted from the question of resource allocation at the margin and the relative rewards of factors and values of products to that of total employment and income. By making a few simple but far-reaching assumptions, Keynes appears to overcome the main obstacles which had blocked the analysis of " involuntary unemployment ". Thus aggregate income (i. e. factor cost plus profit) represents the proceeds of a given employment as well as the supply price of the corresponding output. " . . . in a given situation of technique, resources and factor cost per unit of employment ", says Keynes, " the amount of employment, both in each individual firm and industry and in the aggregate, depends on the amount of proceeds which the entrepreneurs expect to receive from the corresponding output . . . entrepreneurs will endeavor to fix the amount of employment at the level which they expect to maximize the excess of the proceeds over factor cost." [1] The aggregate demand price of a given output, however, may not be equal to the supply price. For when aggregate income (employment) increases, aggregate consumption increases, but not by as much as income. There is a gap between the aggregate supply price of a given output and consumer expenditure on that output. Unless this gap is closed either by an increase in the propensity to consume or by an increase in the rate of current investment, " the economic system may find itself at stable equilibrium . . . at a level below full employment." [2] There is no necessary equality between the demand price of output as a whole and the supply price of that output.

This is the crux of Keynes' theory of underemployment equilibrium. The remainder of the General Theory is concerned chiefly with an analysis of the relationships which underlie this relatively simple structure. In summary form: " . . . given what we shall call the community's propensity to consume, the equilibrium level of employment, i. e. the level at which there is no inducement to employers as a whole either to expand or contract employment, will depend on the amount of current investment. The amount of current investment will depend, in turn, on what we shall call the inducement to invest;

---

1 J. M. Keynes, *The General Theory of Interest and Money Employment*, (New York, Harcourt, 1936), pp. 24-25.

2 *Ibid.*, p. 30.

and the inducement to invest will be found to depend on the relation between the schedule of the marginal efficiency of capital and the complex of rates of interest on loans of various maturities." [3]

Keynes accepted traditional marginal analysis—maximization of returns at the margin—as he did supply-demand analysis.[4] But he completely reoriented these tools of equilibrium analysis by introducing the consumption function and by concentrating his analysis on income determination. The level of employment, and income, is given by the point of intersection of the aggregate supply price (of an employment) and the aggregate demand price, composed of consumption and investment components. Even a familiar concept like that of the marginal efficiency of capital receives new emphasis at his hands as " the factor through which the expectation of changes in the value of money influences the volume of current investment ".[5] The notion of liquidity preference is adapted from the cash balance approach and converted into an analysis of transactions balances whose magnitude depends on income and other accumulated balances. Keynes' emphasis on expectations and the role of money is not new. The Swedish economists and Keynes' associates at Cambridge had gone into the " monetary " problem extensively long before the General Theory made its appearance. The view that Keynes' work did not effect a revolution in economic thought, that he reassembled established concepts and relations, is not altogether unjustified.[6] We encounter familiar concepts and relations

3 *Ibid.*, p. 28.

4 *Ibid.*, Preface, VII " ... our method of analyzing the economic behaviour of the present under the influence of changing ideas about the future ", writes Keynes. "is one which depends on supply and demand, and is, in this way linked up with our fundamental theory of value."

5 *Ibid.*, p. 141.

6 *Cf.* J. R. Hicks, " The Theory of Employment ", *Economic Journal*, 1936, p. 238.

throughout the General Theory, but they have been woven together in a manner which yields an unique theoretical structure.

CHANGES IN TOTAL OUTPUT

The fusion, in the General Theory, of traditional (static) notions with dynamic ones has left a trail of controversy in the literature. Keynes' treatment of output as a whole follows static lines in that the stock of capital assets is taken as fixed along with given preferences and technique. On the supply side changes in total output result from the application of different amounts of employment (wage-units) to the given stock of capital assets where total output is the sum of the employments given by individual entrepreneurs in attempting to maximize their proceeds over factor cost. Yet changes in the scale of output, i. e. employment, seem to be governed on the demand side by changes in expectations which largely determine investment decisions and the level of employment. Keynes deals at considerable length with the factors which influence expectations and the scale of new capital investment. In fact, the General Theory is concerned primarily with the conditions which influence aggregate (effective) demand through the consumption and investment components of output and real income.

One explanation of the emphasis on changes in expectations and investment in an analysis where resources and technique are taken as fixed may be that Keynes was merely exploring factors which influence investment at a point in time. In his theory, the conditions which govern investment over the short-run are given by fairly simple schedule relations. But the most interesting problems center around the complex circumstances which affect the equilibrium level of investment. When employment increases, an equilibrium level will be reached only if that proportion of increased income which is not spent on consumption finds its way into investment outlets. The conditions which govern changes in investment activity are highly relevant to the analysis of equilibrium at a point in time.

This interpretation does not meet the issue entirely. There is a dynamic core in Keynes' treatment of the marginal efficiency of capital and the state of long-run expectations—an element not explained by the given factors—which is not fully compatible with his short-run analysis at a point in time. He refers at numerous points to the fact that it is the prospective rate of return that dominates the marginal efficiency of capital. And he speaks frequently of changes in the prospective yield of capital, of " new investment " [7] brought about by changes in expectations, and the precariousness of the expectations on which the current rate of investment depends. Far from suggesting a point of rest, the impression gained from many passages in the General Theory is one of constant pressure toward change in the rate of investment and the level of employment. " The mistake of regarding the marginal efficiency of capital primarily in terms of the *current* yield of capital equipment, which would be correct only in the static state where there is no changing future to influence the present," says Keynes, "has had the result of breaking the theoretical link between today and tomorrow. Even the rate of interest is, virtually, a current phenomenon; and if we reduce the marginal efficiency of capital to the same status, we cut ourselves off from taking any direct account of the future in our analysis of the existing equilibrium." [8] Keynes' theory of employment may be basically static, but a dynamic element has slipped in which is not explained by the given factors, or by Keynes' independent variables.

This impression seems to be confirmed by other basic features of the General Theory of Employment, Interest and Money. Keynes visualized his theory of employment in part as an analysis of a shifting equilibrium and not merely a (static) equilibrium at a point in time. He tells us most specifically, when he contrasts the Treatise on Money with the

7 *Ibid.*, *cf.*, pp. 29, 142, 165.

8 *Ibid.*, pp. 145-146.

General Theory, that he is seeking to advance a theory of changes in output as a whole: "... the dynamic development, as distinct from the instananeous picture, was left incomplete and extremely confused. This book, on the other hand, has evolved into what is primarily a study of the forces which determine changes in the scale of output and employment as a whole ... " [9] Again he writes, " So long as we limit ourselves to the study of the individual industry or firm on the assumption that the aggregate quantity of employed resources is constant, and, provisionally, that the conditions of other industries or firms are unchanged, it is true that we are not concerned with the significant characteristics of money. But as soon as we pass to the problem of what determines output and employment as a whole, we require the complete theory of a Monetary Economy." [10] He contrasts the two types of analysis further when he says, " ... we might make our line of division between the theory of stationary equilibrium and the theory of shifting equilibrium—meaning by the latter the theory of a system in which changing views about the future are capable of influencing the present situation." [11] Changing views about the future are reflected through the marginal efficiency of capital and here Keynes makes the distinction between,

> ... an additional quantity of capital in the *existing* situation, and the series of increments which it is expected to obtain *over the whole life* of the additional capital asset; —i. e. the distinction between Q_1 and the complete series $Q_1, Q_2, \ldots Q_r \ldots$ This involves the whole question of the place of expectation in economic theory. Most discussions of the marginal efficiency of capital seem to pay no attention to any member of the series except Q_1. Yet this cannot be legitimate except in a static theory, for which all the Q's are equal. The ordinary theory

9 Preface, p. vii.

10 *Ibid.*, p. 293.

11 *Ibid.*, p. 294.

of distribution, where it is assumed that capital is getting *now* its marginal productivity (in some sense or other), is only valid in a stationary state.[12]

But changes in total output and income, to repeat, are supposed to occur in a particular way in Keynes' theory of under-employment equilibrium. " The fluctuations in real income under consideration in this book ", writes Keynes, " are those which result from applying different quantities of employment (i. e., of labour-units) to a given capital equipment so that real income increases and decreases with the number of labour units employed." [13] That is, an increase in total output (and income) is brought about by applying increased quantities of employment to unused (existing) capital resources which are available when there is less than full-employment. But if an increase in output (and income) is to be maintained, there must be an amount of new investment corresponding to the excess of newly realized income over consumption. " . . . the increased employment will prove unprofitable unless there is an increase in investment to fill the gap." [14] Keynes' analysis seems to be static, i. e. assumes a given capital equipment, when he is dealing with aggregate supply price. Here entrepreneurs determine the level of output by applying more or fewer labor units to the given equipment. Most of his analysis, however, is concerned with aggregate demand conditions where an increase in output (and income), originating on the supply side, is maintained only if there is increased (investment) demand for capital assets, i. e. an increase in the amount of capital equipment.

This dual aspect—the assumption of a stationary state and at the same time conditions which make for a shifting equilibrium—occurs throughout the General Theory.[15] There is a

12 *Ibid.*, pp. 138-139.

13 *Ibid.*, p. 114.

14 *Ibid.*, p. 98.

15 Professor Pigou has remarked on this score that " . . . throughout the main part of his (Keynes') book he suggests that some new investment

suggestion of periods in the course of which the equilibrium level of investment and employment shifts.[16] But changes in investment resulting from variable long-term expectations do not lead to a period analysis if we follow Keynes' thoughts on expectations to their conclusion. It would seem, in fact, that Keynes regarded long-term expectations as indeterminate forces having a rather arbitrary effect on investment over the short-run. For " it is of the nature of long-term expectations ", wrote Keynes, " that they cannot be checked at short intervals in the light of realized results ... they are liable to sudden revision." [17]Far from constituting a flaw in his analysis (for which he has been much criticized), Keynes' treatment of long-term expectations appears to spring from his view that there are forces which cannot be fitted into a short-run equilibrium analysis. These long-run forces make investment in a system of private enterprise a jerky, uneven affair. They give us the outlines of a theory of business fluctuations in which the upward movements in business activity and their turning points spring from sudden spurts or deficiencies in investment activity.

Long-Term Expectations

Keynes' discussion of long-term expectations as the basic factor governing current investment through the marginal efficiency of capital has been subject to much criticism. He has been charged with failing to explain how expectations grow out of past experience—of prices, state of demand, cost, profits,

---

is being undertaken every year. It is evident that if this is happening, capital equipment cannot remain unchanged. He is assuming in fact a stationary state and at the same time a moving one." Parenthesis inserted. A. C. Pigou, " Theory of Employment, Interest and Money," Economica, May, 1936, p. 122.

16 The notion of a shifting equilibrium would require the use of a period analysis. The closest that Keynes gets to the specific notion of periods is in his discussion of the income concept where he speaks of "equipment inherited from the previous period" which must be deducted in order to arrive at income of the current period. Op. cit., pp. 52, 62.

17 Ibid., p. 51.

etc.—and how past experience is linked with current production, consumption and investment through the state of expectation. In the Keynesian analysis expectations are frequently open to arbitrary influences, they change spontaneously, and they include a number of factors which cannot be explained on economic grounds.[18]

Yet it is here that Keynes' intuition may have been as penetrating as in other instances in which he has received the tribute of economic theorists. The state of long-term expectation in Keynes' analysis does not correspond to the notion of expectation found in the work of the Swedish economists or that of Hicks and other theorists who assume that expectations, even though uncertain, are somehow formed on the basis of past (economic) experience. Capital investment does not enter into the scheme of price fluctuations discussed by Hicks. We form " probability " estimates of the future in terms of past and current price experience. On the other hand, Keynes' concept of long-term expectations implies a type of uncertainty that is bound up with the process of capital accumulation " for an indefinitely postponable future ". In this case expectations can hardly be referred to as estimates of the future; and this is perhaps why Keynes insisted over and over again on pointing out that expectations are formed on a precarious basis and cannot be rigidly interpreted as probability estimates. The process of capital investment means that wealth must be held in illiquid form for an indefinite period during which capital values may fluctuate for a number of unpredictable reasons.

Keynes clearly identifies the principal influences acting on the marginal efficiency of capital with the state of long-term expectation. Short-term expectation, writes Keynes, " is concerned with the price which a manufacturer can expect to get for his "finished " output at the time when he commits himself

18 Cf. Gottfried Haberler, op. cit., pp. 252-253. Keynes has also been criticized by the Swedish economists for his failure to develop the problem of expectations in terms of expected and realized results. Cf. Eric Lundberg, op. cit., pp. 178-180, Bertil Ohlin, op. cit., pp. 128-130.

to starting the process which will produce it " [19] *with existing plant.* On the other hand, long-term expectation " is concerned with what the entrepreneur can hope to earn in the shape of future returns if he purchases (or, perhaps, manufactures) ' finished ' output as an addition to his capital equipment." [20] Thus in the case of additions to capital equipment, " the producer's short-term expectations are based on the current long-term expectations of the investor ; and it is of the nature of long-term expectations that they cannot be checked at short intervals in the light of realized results." [21] Expectations are the link between the short-run with its given conditions and fairly limited horizons and long-run developments which are not foreseeable with any degree of accuracy. Long-run expectations reflect the uncertainty which springs from the accumulation of wealth in the present for an indefinite period in the future. Investment is a hazardous affair because the purchase of capital assets represents a claim to prospective yield which may be adversely (or favorably) affected by a variety of factors arising during the life of the asset. Increased capital accumulation lowers the marginal efficiency of capital because prospective yield falls as the supply of a capital asset increases. Prospective yield from given equipment falls too if changes in prospective costs are expected, i. e. as a result of lowered labor-cost, inventions, and new technique or even changes in the political and social atmosphere. Many of the factors which may affect the marginal efficiency of capital and the prospective yield from investment, as discussed by Keynes, are not " economic " in the sense in which the term is used in equilibrium analysis.

Keynes, for example, deals with the question of " confidence ", or the reliability with which expectations are formed and forecasts made. But he does not surround the notion with the vagueness which it usually has in the current literature on

19 Keynes, *op. cit.*, pp. 46, 148.

20 *Ibid.*, pp. 46-47.

21 *Ibid.*, p. 51.

expectations. He discusses it in terms of forces which most economists trained in traditional equilibrium analysis would regard as "non-economic". Investment activity and "economic prosperity", writes Keynes, "is excessively dependent on a political and social atmosphere which is congenial to the average business man. If the fear of a Labour Government or a New Deal depresses enterprise, this need not be the result of a reasonable calculation or of a plot with political intent; —it is the mere consequence of upsetting the delicate balance of spontaneous optimism." [22] There is a large measure of chance, spontaneous optimism and irrationality associated with expectations of prospective yield which cannot be divorced from the conditions under which private investment activity is conducted. Even the organization of modern investment markets around conventional norms—the view that " the existing state of affairs will continue indefinitely except insofar as we have reasons to expect a change " [23]—is a precarious thing at best. This " convention " gives the individual investor a degree of liquidity by enabling him to revise his judgments and change his investments over a succession of short-run periods. But this does not afford " liquidity " of investment for the community as a whole. Moreover, the separation of ownership and management in organized investment markets has substantially increased the precariousness of the investment process. Real knowledge in the valuation of assets has declined and day-to-day fluctuations in returns, or transactions in which immediate profits can be made, tend to have an exaggerated influence on investment activity.

When all is said, there is a large element of chance in private investment decisions and, consequently, " the volume of investment is unplanned and uncontrolled, subject to the vagaries of the marginal efficiency of capital as determined by the private judgment of individuals ignorant or speculative

22 *Ibid.*, p. 162.
23 *Ibid.*, p. 152.

and to a long-term rate of interest which seldom falls below a conventional level." [24] There is no escaping the conclusion that Keynes did not think it possible to develop a determinate explanation of changing expectations within the context of a short-run analysis. Expectations refer, in part, to long-run events and, in part, to existing political and social conditions which affect investment decisions quite apart from the customary (given) factors in conventional equilibrium analysis. The precarious basis on which estimates of prospective yield are formed is characteristic of the private investment process and makes expectations, and the scale of investment, subject to "sudden revision". Keynes' discussion of expectations suggests factors which may be indeterminate within the framework of equilibrium analysis but crucial to the problem of unemployment and economic fluctuations in a system of private enterprise.

Long-run forces which influence investment decisions through the marginal efficiency of capital are discussed by Keynes at scattered points throughout the General Theory. Though his comments on this score are brief and rather perfunctory asides on his main theme—determination of the scale of investment over the short-run in a given state of wealth and income distribution—they give us glimpses of some of the historical conditions which make for the contemporary insufficiency of private investment.

Keynes, for example, contrasts the present-day level of the marginal efficiency of capital with that which prevailed during the nineteenth century. In the latter period, Keynes writes

> ... the growth of population and of invention, the opening-up of new lands, the state of confidence and the frequency of war over the average (say) of each decade seem to have been sufficient, taken in conjunction with the propensity to consume, to establish a reasonably satisfactory average level of

24 *Ibid.*, pp. 324-325.

employment to be compatible with a rate of interest high enough to be psychologically acceptable to wealth-owners.[25]

In the absence of the favorable opportunities for investment which formerly prevailed, the marginal efficiency of capital today has fallen to a point where a reasonable average level of employment would require an average rate of interest unacceptable to wealth-owners. The minimum rate of interest acceptable to wealth-owners generally is too stable to be altered merely by manipulating the quantity of money. The result is a deficient scale of investment. We have here a broad reference to the historical conditions which govern the (prospective) yield from investment over the long run and the conflict between fixed returns and investment returns from capital assets which breeds unemployment.

In his notes on mercantilism Keynes mentions another long-run factor which conditions the marginal efficiency of capital and the scale of new investment. Here he suggests that the weakness of the inducement to invest " may chiefly lie in the extent of existing accumulations " of capital; whereas, formerly, " risks and hazards of all kinds may have played a larger part ".[26] Thus the marginal efficiency of capital in present-day conditions may be largely dominated by the pressure on prospective yield resulting from a greatly increased supply of capital assets of various types. This thesis—that capital accumulation has reached an advanced stage in contemporary society with a consequently lowered marginal efficiency of capital relative to the rate of interest—recurs throughout Keynes' discussion.[27]

Above all, the existing inequality of wealth and income provide the background for Keynes' discussion of the contemporary problem of securing sufficient investment. Keynes suggests that among " the outstanding faults of the economic society in which we live are its... arbitrary and inequitable

25 *Ibid.*, p. 307.

26 *Ibid.*, p. 348.

27 *Ibid.*, Ch. XVI, especially pp. 217, 219-220.

distribution of wealth and incomes." [28] An inequitable distribution of income holds down the propensity to consume and, up to the point where full employment is realized, retards effective demand and the growth of capital. There is an even more significant point which bears on the inequality of wealth. In the Keynesian theory of employment the extent of effective saving is determined by the scale of investment which, in turn, is promoted by a low rate of interest. The inducement to accumulate wealth through a high rate of interest ultimately retards, rather than increases the accretion of new wealth. " One of the chief social justifications of great inequality of wealth," concludes Keynes, " is, therefore, removed." [29]

Keynes was unquestionably aware of the historical implications of his analysis : the fact that the contemporary situation must be carefully distinguished from other periods in the development of the private enterprise system. In contrast to traditional (static) theory and temporary equilibrium analysis with their timeless exchange relations, the General Theory of Employment reflects the historical circumstances of its period. Though general in character, Keynes' references to long-run factors which affect the inducement to invest and the propensity to consume impart a high degree of realism to his analysis of underemployment equilibrium in the short run. These references suggest the decisive forces even though they do not provide us with an adequate account of their interaction over the long run.

This brings us to another aspect of Keynes' theory of employment which has been much criticized. Keynes did not consider the problem of monopoly which is, after all, closely related to under-utilization of resources both in the form of unemployed labor and unused plant and equipment. On the other hand, Keynes develops his analysis of unemployment against the background of inequality of wealth and income

28 *Ibid.*, p. 372.

29 *Ibid.*, p. 373.

which is fostered and deepened by monopoly conditions. He discusses these conditions, only briefly as we have seen; but there is ample evidence that inequalities of wealth and income are one of the central issues of policy in the General Theory. Moreover, his discussion of the precariousness of expectations in a system of private enterprise gives us important clues to the behavior of monopolistic elements in our society. Monopoly seems indeed to deepen the problems which beset the modern enterprise economy by increasing the distortion of income distribution, by maintaining rigid prices, and especially by adopting restrictive practices with respect to new capital investment. Monopolistic restrictions on investment seem to be very well described in Keynes' discussion of the depressing effect on prospective yield of an already large accumulation of capital and of expected changes in technique. But before these factors can be applied in dynamic theory, they have to be brought within the scope of theory in a systematic way. A theory like Keynes', which is primarily directed at a specific problem— underemployment equilibrium—cannot be expected to do everything. It offers many suggestive possibilities for a realistic theoretical analysis of the central problem of our period: the failure to provide sufficient sustained employment at a high level of output and national income.

KEYNES ON THE TRADE CYCLE

Keynes' theory of employment has contributed immeasurably to the development of new areas of business cycle research and theory. Statistical studies of income have been in progress for many years. But the General Theory of Employment gave the concept of national income a significance that it did not have before and stimulated fresh lines of attack on the problem. A tentative theory of the business cycle, developed initially by Harrod, owes much to Keynes, especially to his concept of the consumption function. In addition, the General Theory contains a number of suggestive comments both in the discussion of the theory of employment proper and in Keynes' notes on the trade cycle. These comments do not constitute anything like a systematic theory of the cycle and are in the nature of penetrating conjectures rather than hypotheses reasoned from empirical evidence. But they provide important insights into the problem.

Keynes does not take the narrow view that fluctuations in investment and in the marginal efficiency of capital merely occur spasmodically but believes that such fluctuations can take place with some degree of regularity. " We do not merely mean by a *cyclical* movement ", writes Keynes, " that upward and downward tendencies, once started, do not persist for ever in the same direction but are ultimately reversed. We mean also that there is some recognizable degree of regularity in the time-sequence and duration of the upward and downward movements." [30] Yet this view is in sharp contrast to Keynes' frequent assertion at other points in the General Theory that the upper turning point of the cycle is dominated chiefly by " sudden and violent changes " in the marginal efficiency of capital. In Keynes' discussion of the cycle these changes remain rather arbitrary and irregular reactions to shifts in prospective yield. It is only in his discussion of the lower turning point that he suggests a factor which may impart a certain order of regularity to changes in the marginal efficiency of capital. In short, Keynes does not provide an explanation of " the time-sequence and duration " of the cycle in its full course.

Keynes at one point observes that a period of rapid capital expansion is accompanied by the provision for sinking funds and depreciation allowances on a scale so far in excess of current requirements for repair and renewal that there is not enough new investment to take up both these funds and new current saving. It is this type of " ' financial prudence ' " which, following a " lively burst of investment in long-lived capital ", may be sufficient to cause a slump.[31] This is the familiar

30 Keynes, *op. cit.*, p. 314.

31 *Ibid.*, p. 100.

theme of over-saving. But it seems to be merely an aside. Keynes finds the chief explanation of the upper turning point of the cycle in sudden revisions in expectations. " . . . we have been accustomed ", he says, " in explaining the ' crisis ' to lay stress on the rising tendency of the rate of interest under the influence of the increased demand for money both for trade and speculative purposes. At times this factor may certainly play an aggravating and, occasionally perhaps, an initiating part. But I suggest that a more typical, and often predominant, explanation of the crisis, is not primarily a rise in the rate of interest, but a sudden collapse in the marginal efficiency of capital." [32] The reason for this collapse is not given in any great detail. It results from the fact that current expectations of future yield are based on unreliable evidence and are subject to sudden and violent changes; organized investment markets are under the influence of purchasers who are ignorant of what they are buying and of speculators who are little concerned with reasonable estimates of future yield; and current yield shows signs of falling off as the stock of newly-produced capital goods increases. The collapse in the marginal efficiency of capital is associated with an increase in liquidity-preference and the rate of interest which aggravate the decline in investment, but this occurs only after the collapse has taken place. Despite Keynes' mention of systematic factors which govern the collapse of the marginal efficiency of capital, these factors do not explain " regularity in the time-sequence and duration of the upward and downward movements " of the business cycle.

Keynes suggests that recovery from the slump is a result of the fact that capital-assets have different ages, wear out with time, and do not have a very long life. If the rate of investment falls below a certain minimum, " it is merely a question of time (failing large fluctuations in other factors) before the marginal efficiency of capital rises sufficiently to bring about a recovery of investment above this minimum." [33] Keynes sug-

32 *Ibid.*, p. 315.

33 *Ibid.*, p. 253.

gests that a second factor governing the length of the down-turn is the time required to reduce surplus stocks of unfinished goods. Keynes conceives that these two factors, acting together, provide an explanation of the fairly regular time-period required for recovery from the depression.

> The explanation of the *time-element* in the trade cycle, of the fact that an interval of time of a particular order of magnitude must usually elapse before recovery begins, is to be sought in the influences which govern the recovery of the marginal efficiency of capital. There are reasons, given firstly by the length of life of durable assets in relation to the normal rate of growth in a given epoch, and secondly by the carrying-costs of surplus stocks, why the duration of the downward movement should have an order of magnitude which is not fortuitous, which does not fluctuate between, say, one year this time and ten years next time, but which shows some regularity between, let us say, three and five years.[34]

Keynes even ventures the opinion that capital may have an average durability in a given epoch and that the " standard time-interval " required to produce a shortage of capital will change if the characteristics of the epoch shift. He does not elaborate on what he means by the characteristics of an epoch, but speaks merely of changes in the growth of the population and in what he terms the " normal rate of growth " of durable assets.

Keynes notes too that fluctuations in inventories play a part in causing " the minor oscillations within the main movement of the Trade Cycle." [35] But he does not indicate just how these fluctuations in inventories are to be fitted in with his suggestion that reduction of the carrying-costs of surplus stocks— on hand when new investment suddenly ceases—is one of the factors which imparts some regularity to the duration of the down-turn. Presumably one reference is to stocks carried over from

34 *Ibid.*, p. 317.

35 *Ibid.*, p. 332.

a high level of investment activity which has come to a stop, while the other applies to stocks arising from miscalculations in estimating the scale of consumption over short periods. But we are not told whether the second type of change in inventories is independent of or related to the first except for the hint that they both affect the current rate of investment.

KEYNESIAN BUSINESS CYCLE THEORY

A theory of the business cycle based on Keynes' work has been developed by Harrod [36] and stated in more rigorous form by Hansen [37] and Samuelson.[38] This theory attempts to combine Keynes' multiplier relation with the acceleration principle into an explanation of turning points in the level of economic activity. Keynes views the multiplier as a combination of an income equation and a " fairly stable " consumption function [39] obeying a definite psychological law : as income increases (as a result of new investment) the marginal and average propensities to consume fall and the marginal propensity is always less than unity. The marginal propensity to consume " . . . tells us how the next increment of output will have to be divided between consumption and investment." [40] It is this relation between net investment, real income and consumption which

36 R. F. Harrod, *The Trade Cycle* (Oxford: Oxford University Press, 1936).

37 Alvin H. Hansen, *Fiscal Policy and Business Cycles* (New York: Norton, 1941).

38 Paul A. Samuelson, " Interactions between the Acceleration Principle and the Multiplier," *Review of Economic Statistics*, May, 1939, pp. 75-78. Same Author, "A Synthesis of the Principle of Acceleration and the Multiplier," *Journal of Political Economy*, December, 1939, pp. 786-797.

39 *Cf.* Richard M. Goodwin, " The Multiplier," *The New Economics* (New York: Knopf, 1947), p. 485. Professor Haberler has observed that Keynes confuses a formal relation with an empirical relation in making his " psychological law " of consumption interchangeable with the multiplier. Gottfried Haberler, " Mr. Keynes' Theory of the Multiplier," *Readings in Business Cycle Theory*, pp. 195 ff.

40 J. M. Keynes, *op. cit.*, p. 315.

has been linked with the acceleration principle. The consumption function alone cannot explain turning points in the cycle.[41] The fact that consumption expenditure does not increase as rapidly as income must be related to some factor which governs general economic activity in order to explain why an expansion comes to an end. The principle of acceleration is the basis of such a relation. It postulates a relation between the rate of change of consumer demand and the derived demand for producer goods, namely that, once started, a decrease or increase in the rate of growth of consumer demand is self-perpetuating. A moderate decrease, writes J. M. Clark,

> in the rate of growth of consumer demand ... may result—with a lag—in a positive decline in the rate of production of durable producers' or consumers' goods. This in turn reduces purchasing power, unless offset by opposite movements elsewhere, and results in a positive decrease in consumers' demand, presumably extended to more commodities than those originally affected. And this in turn further extends and intensifies the shrinkage in production of durable goods, etc.[42]

The multiplier, given in terms of the consumption function, explains how a decrease in the rate of growth of consumer demand originates. The acceleration principle explains how this decrease starts a decline in investment activity which reinforces the original decrease in the rate of growth of consumption. Taken together, these two relations suggest a reasonable ex-

---

41 Metzler suggests that the consumption function explains turning points when he notes that cumulative movements cannot go on indefinitely because consumption expenditure increases less rapidly than income and falls less rapidly than income. Lloyd A. Metzler, "Keynes and the Theory of the Business Cycle," *The New Economics*, pp. 438, 440-441. This implies that investment outlets are insufficient to absorb a rising proportion of current savings as income rises i. e. that no new net investment is undertaken independently of the current volume of consumption. But the initial rise in income, supplied by new investment, is missing and leaves this explanation incomplete.

42 J. M. Clark, "Capital Production and Consumer-Taking: A Further Word," *Journal of Political Economy*, October, 1932, pp. 692-693.

planation of fluctuations in the general level of economic activity. The theory based on the interaction of the two relations explains how fluctuations originate within the economic system, rather than from limiting factors which act on the economic system, and why there are turning points in the level of economic activity. It even explains why fluctuations recur. A downturn in economic activity will be checked because consumer demand falls less rapidly than real income. At some point in the contraction the less rapid decline in consumer demand relative to the fall in real income will set the stage for a revival of new investment activity. This starts the upturn in economic activity and sets the stage for an expansion which will come to an end when the slackened rate of growth in consumer demand results in intensified fluctuations in capital investment and a self-perpetuating decrease in income and consumption. While this theory suggests a reason for recurrence of fluctuations, it does not, of course, explain why the upturn and downturn in economic activity have a fairly definite order of duration.

The theory of the cycle based on a synthesis of the multiplier and the acceleration principle has been modified substantially since it was first formulated by Harrod. The cycle, according to Harrod, results from the joint action of the multiplier and principle of acceleration (Relation) working through three dynamic determinants: (1) the propensity to save, (2) the shift to profit, and (3) the amount of capital used in production. The first determinant depends on the principle that the amount of saving is accommodated to the amount of net investment through changes in the level of income (the multiplier). The second determinant explains why variations in total income are not wholly proportional to variations in net investment and saving. The third determinant is concerned with the tendency of production to become more capitalistic in the boom, in part because of inventions and technological change.

The three determinants set the course of the expansion phase of the cycle in the following way. First, as net investment increases and incomes rise, people tend to save a larger proportion of income. Second, there is a shift toward profits during the upward movement, a fact that reinforces the tendency for savings to increase proportionately more as income rises. The redistribution of income " in proportions more favorable to profit in the boom and less favorable in the slump " [43] is fundamental to Harrod's theory because profit-receivers are important savers. This shift toward profits takes place in accordance with the principle of diminishing returns and the diminishing elasticity of demand as output rises. " If profit per unit of output becomes greater or less ", writes Harrod, " either the excess of price over marginal revenue must become greater or less or the difference between marginal cost and average cost must change in the appropriate way... this does not depend on any particular theory of the trade cycle but solely on the assumption that the entrepreneur is trying to maximize profit." [44] The law of diminishing returns accounts both for a rise of prices and a shift to profits, i.e. as output increases, marginal cost and prices rise, while a shift to profits occurs if the ratio of marginal costs to average costs is rising. The greater the shift to profits, the smaller the increase in consumption in terms of the action of the multiplier, resulting from a given increase in net investment. The tendency of production to become more capitalistic (third determinant) during the boom tends to offset the restrictive influence of the first two determinants. But the shift to profits as output increases, coupled with the fact there is a tendency to save a larger proportion of a higher income, means that a point is reached where a given rate of increase of net investment no longer proves justified and the rate of increase of investment tends to slow down. This leads to a further slowing down in

43 Harrod, *op. cit.*, p. 78.
44 *Loc. cit.*

the rate of increase of income and consumption. From this point on, the Relation, as Harrod terms the acceleration principle, induces an absolute fall in net investment. This results in a further fall in the level of income and consumption, causing a decline in the level of investment to that required for replacements.[45]

Harrod's discussion of the cycle is confined principally to the expansion phase and to an explanation of the upper turning point. He does not explain the depression and lower turning point in the same terms as the boom and downturn. When the bottom of the depression is reached, " revival is likely to come ", says Harrod, because " ... the mere passage of time increases the amount of replacements required to maintain a given level of output. This increase involves a rise of net investment " [46] and sets the stage for the operation of the three dynamic determinants and the start of another upward, cumulative advance.

This theory of the cycle has been put in a more rigorous form by Hansen and Samuelson. In a modified version of the theory Hansen breaks up the additions to national income into three parts: [47] governmental deficit spending, private consumption expenditure induced by previous public expenditure, and induced private investment, assumed to be proportional to the time increase of consumption. Samuelson has developed model

45 In an article published subsequent to his book on the trade cycle, Harrod suggests that the acceleration principle has a more limited influence on an expansion. Harrod notes that " Some outlays of capital have no direct relation to the current increase of output", but " ... may be related to a prospective long-period increase of activity ... or they may be induced by new inventions calculated to cheapen production ... " R. F. Harrod, "An Essay in Dynamic Theory," *Economic Journal*, March, 1939, p. 26. The larger the volume of outlay sustained independently of the current rate of growth of output, the smaller the proportion of savings which will have to be " looked after by the acceleration principle."

46 *Ibid.*, p. 101.

47 *Cf.* Samuelson's reference to Hansen's work, " Interaction between the Multiplier Analysis and the Principle of Acceleration," *loc. cit.*

sequences, based on different numerical values of the multiplier and acceleration principle, which illustrate this scheme. Using four selected pairs of values for the multiplier and the acceleration coefficient, Samuelson covers the different possible qualitative types of behavior of the two combined relations. Samuelson found that for the marginal propensity to consume equal to one-half and the acceleration coefficient equal to one, an expansion must lead to a downturn, even without the action of Harrod's two dynamic determinants. For any given value of the propensity to consume, small values of the acceleration coefficient yield merely asymptotic approaches to stationary equilibrium. For the same value of the multiplier and slightly larger values for the acceleration coefficient, the result is cyclical oscillations which become smaller and smaller. Very large values for the acceleration coefficient lead to explosive cumulative movements growing at a compound interest rate, indicating that the fact that the marginal propensity to consume is always less than unity is not sufficient to lead to a downturn or to the end of a cumulative movement. However, if the assumption of linearity of the consumption function is dropped, and the marginal propensity to consume allowed to approach zero in the limit, any disequilibrating cumulative movement will be reversed. Samuelson's conclusion is important: the average level of the economic system is independent of the operation of the acceleration principle and depends rather on the level of investment outlets.[48]

SHORT-RUN *versus* LONG-RUN FACTORS IN INVESTMENT ACTIVITY

In the theory of the cycle based on a synthesis of the multiplier analysis and the acceleration principle the originating cause of fluctuations in business activity is the failure of consumption to keep up with income as the latter rises. As Hansen has observed, the theory rests on the assumption that no new

[48] Samuelson, "A Synthesis of the Principle of Acceleration and the Multiplier," *op. cit.*, pp. 793-795.

net investment is undertaken independently of the current volume of consumption. An increment of investment generates an increase in income and consumption. This induces further investment in an expansion which must come to an end because consumption does not keep pace with the increase in income. In other words, people save a larger proportion of their income as incomes rise and, with capital investment wholly dependent on the rate of increase of consumer demand, the scale of investment will slacken as higher levels of income (and saving) are reached. Over the long run, however, new investment is actually based only in part, or even very slightly, on the volume of current consumption. " Thus, net investment," writes Hansen, " is fundamentally a function of factors lying quite outside of the current volume of consumption or the current volume of income. . . . In the absence of new investment outlets adequate to maintain the boom, it is clear that any continued volume of investment, such as would be necessary to maintain income at a full level, would rapidly experience a drastic fall in the prospective rate of profit on new investment. . . ." [49] But the fact that savings grow as income increases—on the assumption of a stable consumption function —does not mean that savings merely accumulate and do not find investment outlets. The availability of investment outlets seems to be the factor which mainly determines the level of consumption expenditures through the generation of income rather than the other way round. There is mutual interaction between the two sets of factors—between new investment and increased current consumption which may stimulate additional secondary investment—but, in general, new investment activity does not seem to be primarily dependent on the volume of current consumption.

49 Hansen, *op. cit.*, pp. 287-288. Hansen, of course, sees the contemporary problem presented by a stable consumption function as one " . . . of limited investment outlets—outlets inadequate to fill the gap fixed by the consumption-savings pattern . . . " *Ibid.*, p. 248.

What then are the factors, other than current demand for consumer goods, which govern the rate of new investment? Investment is a long-term affair. It represents a commitment to keep wealth in illiquid form for a considerable period of time and to receive periodic returns whose value may fluctuate considerably over the life of an asset. Professor D. H. Robertson suggests long-term factors which motivate new investment when he writes: " . . . Some of the principal forms of investment in the modern world—the instruments of power production, of transport, of office activity—are, after all, very loosely geared to the visible demand for particular types of consumption goods and depend rather on fairly vague estimates of the future progress of whole areas and populations." [50] Haberler has suggested the term " routine investments " for investments (in working and fixed capital) " which follow more or less clearly the ups and downs of consumer demand ".[51] He contrasts this type of investment with that which looks forward to the very distant future for its utilization and has very little connection with recent movements of demand for consumer goods. Dr. Ezekiel has offered the following classification of types of capital investment: (1) long-term or permanent private investment which includes items of expenditure for all durable capital goods; (2) short-term or temporary private investment of which changes in consumers' credit and in inventories are examples; (3) quasi-investment or investment which is not attributable to the decisions of private individuals and business concerns but reflects institutional transactions summarized by the two categories of net foreign balance and government net contribution.[52] If we limit the combined action of the multiplier and the acceleration principle to the short-run type of

---

50 D. H. Robertson, " Review of Harrod's Trade Cycle," *Canadian Journal of Economics and Political Science*, February, 1937, p. 126.

51 G. Haberler, *Prosperity and Depression*, p. 98.

52 Mordecai Ezekiel, " Saving, Investment and Consumption: II ", *American Economic Review*, June, 1942, p. 274.

investment mentioned by these writers, then the theory of the cycle based on a synthesis of the two relations omits a substantial area of investment activity which has little connection with current consumption.

There is another factor which seriously qualifies the theory of the cycle based on a synthesis of the multiplier and the principle of acceleration. As Dr. Kuznets has observed, it is rather difficult in the short run to distinguish between the need for durable capital for replacement and the demand for durable capital additions. Investment decisions are likely to be made in terms of capital for replacement and capital for new additions combined. Moreover, the capacity of an item of equipment over the short-run is elastic and replacement can be deferred within limits. " When cyclical fluctuations in the cost of equipment and volume of activity are considered ", says Kuznets, " it may be seen that they affect the entrepreneur in his choice as between further retention of old equipment and replacement of it by new units." [53] Unused capacity, the postponable nature of replacements, and the possibility that replacement, say, on account of obsolescence, may result in increased productivity gives the business firm a certain amount of leeway in adjusting to increased consumer demand over the short run. These factors probably provide a way of hedging against increases in consumer demand when additions to plant and equipment might be regarded as risky ventures, e.g., when the increase in demand may not be expected to last.[54]

53 Simon Kuznets, *Economic Essays in Honor of John Bates Clark* (New York: Macmillan, 1927), p. 237. J. M. Clark agrees substantially with the qualifications adduced by Kuznets and notes that he too qualified the acceleration hypothesis in its simplified form. J. M. Clark, "Additional Note on 'Business Acceleration and the Law of Demand,'" Readings in Business Cycle Theory, pp. 256-257.

54 In fact, the announced postwar policy of so important a corporate unit as U. S. Steel has been that demand would probably not continue indefinitely at peak capacity and that reserves would have to be retained in anticipation of a much reduced level of demand and output instead of being used for additions. *Cf.* the statement of Irving S. Olds, *New York Times*, April 30,

Another debatable aspect of the theory based on a synthesis of the multiplier and the acceleration principle concerns the stability of the consumption function. The view that the consumption function is stable—Keynes' psychological law—has been questioned on the grounds that this assigns a passive role to consumption and ties it rather rigidly to income. It is suggested, for example, that secular changes in the consumption function and the possible role of such changes in economic development are overlooked in postulating a stable consumption function.[55] Hansen, Ezekiel and others have presented evidence in support of the view that the consumption function is stable.[56] But the statistical evidence on this score is not conclusive. The volume of savings is dependent not only on the size of the national income but on its distribution. It can be reasoned of course that the prevailing distribution of income, and therefore the pattern of consumption and saving, is fairly stable. It is governed by deep-seated institutional conditions which are normally subject to change only over long periods of time. Differences of opinion regarding the stability of the consumption-saving pattern may depend on rather divergent assumptions as to the social and political feasibility of changes in income distribution.

While it fluctuates substantially, capital accumulation has gone on in good periods and bad.[57] Capital accumulation may

---

1947. This type of problem is bound up with the question of protection of existing investment which forms a separate and perhaps leading chapter in a discussion of factors governing long-run private investment activity.

55 Cf. A. F. Burns, "Keynesian Economics Once Again", Review of Economic Statistics, November, 1947, p. 262. Kuznets' data do not support the assumption of constancy—implicit in Keynesian discussions of the multiplier—in the ratio of changes in investment to changes in income in either the declining or rising phases of business cycles from 1919 to 1938. Simon Kuznets, National Income and its Composition, 1919-1938, pp. 269-271.

56 Hansen, op. cit., pp. 247-249. Mordecai Ezekiel, "Saving, Consumption and Investment, I", American Economic Review, March, 1942, pp. 22-49.

57 Cf. Kuznets' data on capital formation by decades from 1869 to 1938. Simon Kuznets, National Income, A Summary of the Findings (New York: National Bureau of Economic Research, 1946), pp. 52-53.

fluctuate not because investment outlets are insufficient to absorb all the savings people make during a boom, but perhaps
because investment opportunities become *temporarily* reduced
and new ones must be found. There is nothing mechanical
about this process because investment outlets may take many
different forms in a dynamic, changing economy. Consumer
demand is an important factor but in the sense (say) of
changes in the rate of growth of the population and of the
national income which may be anticipated only vaguely by
business men. Other changes which may indirectly govern
the conditions under which investments are made over the
long run might include new technique, the opening up of new
territories, the organization of industry, the bargaining position of labor, government fiscal policy, etc. In short, a theory
of economic development may be a prerequisite to a theory of
cyclical (or other) fluctuations in investment in a system of
private enterprise.[58] The failure to define carefully the long-
run conditions under which investment activity functions in
our society may explain in large part the shortcomings of the
theory of the business cycle based on a synthesis of the acceleration principle and the multiplier.

The suggestions offered by Keynes still challenge the in-
genuity of economists. The rate of return from new investment,
given approximately by the relation between the marginal
efficiency of capital and the rate of interest—a relation which
shifts from one epoch to another—dominates the upper turning point of the cycle. For an explanation of the lower turning

---

58 One of the principal problems facing a theory of economic development
might be the need to determine the characteristics of epochs in capitalist
economy (say) in terms of the conditions listed above, and consideration of
fluctuations in investment within such a setting. In his review of long-term
changes in capital formation in the U. S. economy from 1869 to 1938,
Kuznets suggests factors which governed different stages of growth in the
past. *Ibid.*, pp. 55 ff. While these data are estimates and must be used with
caution, they might, together with other relevant statistical and historical
data, provide a basis for the classification of periods or epochs associated
with different types of capital accumulation and investment outlets.

point we have Keynes' suggestion that technical factors like the durability of capital and the time needed to reduce inventories govern the duration of the depression in terms of restoration of the marginal efficiency of capital to a level leading to an upturn in economic activity. The possibility of developing a theory of turning points based on the relation between durability of capital and the marginal efficiency of capital is intriguing. Keynesian analysis suggests an explanation of cyclical movements in investment activity. But if we seek to advance beyond that analysis to a theory of cyclical fluctuations, we seem to need methods of anaysis that are not confined to the short run.

CHAPTER VI

EMPLOYMENT AND THE DEMAND FOR CAPITAL

OUR examination of contemporary dynamic theories suggests that these do not provide us with a satisfactory theory of the business cycle and of the fluctuations in employment which mark the movements of the cycle. A number of factors that may govern cyclical (or other) fluctuations are suggested by the theories discussed. But these theories are incomplete, in part, it is true, because they are not explicitly concerned with the business cycle, and in part because they fail to explain fluctuations in terms of forces inherent in the system of production and sales. This deficiency seems to spring from the fact that these theories aim at a determinate analysis along traditional lines. While they bring changing expectations into the picture, they do not establish the rigorous causal determination of expectations. Indeed, it becomes quite difficult to explain expectations in terms of what went before when much of the causation lies outside the particular system of explanation.

Despite substantial difference as to theoretical tools, economists are generally agreed that the maintenance of a high level of employment is the principal problem facing the system of private enterprise in the foreseeable future. They are in general agreement too that insufficient demand for capital lies at the heart of the problem. But there is considerable disagreement as to the relative importance of different causes affecting the demand for capital. These differences of view go along with different conceptions of economic policy, especially the extent to which government should itself participate in the investment process or assume social responsibilities which, by increasing the tax burden or by promoting redistribution of income, may curtail the supply of private capital. In dealing with the problem of investment and employment, economic theory cannot hope to rise entirely above contemporary questions of group interest, nor can it suggest measures which are wholly neutral or free of controversial content.

In what follows, we attempt to construct a framework for certain well-known facts by taking investment activity as the key factor governing changes in employment over the long run. We shall examine this problem in terms of the American economy between the two wars. We are not trying to advance an hypothesis of economic development, but to suggest that the problem of cyclical (or other) fluctuations is hardly amenable to study without some reference to a long-run framework. If the demand for capital is accepted as the main variable governing employment, then it does not suffice to trace changes in investment activity to changes in business psychology or in long-run expectations. When we attempt to trace business reactions in this way, we imply some scheme of valuation which the business community follows in undertaking new investment. But the institutional arrangements which underlie this scheme—private ownership of wealth and the accumulation of wealth through production for a market—are simply taken for granted. In considering the long-run demand for capital and its bearing on employment, we may be able to see what these arrangements consist of in a particular setting and how they may give rise to self-generating changes. Conclusions reached are necessarily tentative and exploratory.[1]

1 We do not attempt to employ a model analysis for the following reasons. It is true that the use of mathematical models permits of a certain exactness of analysis in some economic problems. In many cases, however, the complexity of the equations which might be used would defy realistic analysis because of restrictive assumptions. One of these assumptions, namely linearity of the relation expressed between determining and determined variables in an equation, is not often realized in practice. And when linearity is achieved by taking short intervals, we are pretty much restricted to the short run. For another thing, secular change and large oscillations are hardly well-described by the conventional apparatus—the mathematics of (small) marginal change, unless we assume some mechanism of cumulation. Still another limiting assumption, independence of determining variables, rarely holds in economic problems because economics is not a field in which

Some Long-Term Factors Governing Employment

There seem to be at least three principal long-run (dynamic) causes of underemployment in the changed economic setting which emerged after World War I. First, investment activity was closely affected by the new conditions which prevailed in the domestic and world economy. Investment activity took new channels after World War I, when the American economy emerged with a basic capital structure built up during preceding stages of growth. While domestic United States investment was high during the twenties, we find significant changes in the composition of net capital formation as compared with earlier stages of growth. For example, there appears to have been a drop in the share of construction in net capital formation, an increased proportion of investment in producer durable equipment, and a rise in net capital formation of additions to claims against foreign countries. In other words, progressive industrialization of the American economy meant a shift toward increased investment in durable producer goods and, after World War I, substantial export of capital, reflected in the new international creditor position of the United States. Decade estimates indicate an increase from 14 per cent to 22 per cent in the share of producer durable equipment in net capital formation for the period 1869-78 to 1928-38.[2] During the same period the share in net capital formation of additions to claims against foreign countries rose from minus 2.8 per cent to almost 17 per cent of total net capital formation.[3]

---

mechanical forces operate. In fact, interdependence of variables seems to be a characteristic feature of causal connection in economic problems. And the relative importance of each variable may change.

2 Simon Kuznets, *National Income: A Summary of the Findings*, p. 55.

3 *Ibid.* For the period 1919-29, this item amounted to an estimated 16 per cent of net capital formation (at 1929 prices). Simon Kuznets, *National Income and Its Composition, 1919-38*, p. 272. While these are rough estimates at best, they give us orders of magnitude which parallel known historical trends in the industrialization of the American economy and its concurrent rise as a creditor nation. For example, see Chester Wright, *Economic History of the United States*, pp. 666-669, 706-719, 809-811.

What were some of the conditions that accompanied these changes in the composition of United States net capital formation after World War I? Widespread domestic and international cartel arrangements revealed themselves in unused capacity and rigid prices. And heavy investments during the twenties did not lead to price reductions which might presumably have resulted from investment in new equipment under competitive conditions.[4] Similarly, foreign lending by American investors on an unprecedented scale was followed by measures intended to protect the domestic market. Repayment of foreign loans became increasingly difficult as United States import restrictions mounted and other leading industrial nations confronted each other with rising tariff barriers. These conditions complicated the financial problems of borrowers and reduced their standing as good investment risks so that in the wake of the depression of the thirties default on private investments was widespread.

Unstable conditions did not of course uniformly assert their influence on investment activity between the two wars. But the factors making for instability and institutional change were almost constantly in the background in a world tied together more closely than ever before by a network of trade and commercial practices—private and governmental—which reacted sensitively to events in each of the major industrial countries. The predominant characteristic of the world economy from the end of one war to the beginning of the next was profound uncertainty in a world undergoing rapid change, political, social and economic.

Second, there seems to have been considerable substitution of capital for manpower as the latter improved its bargaining position after World War I. There was at least a very close connection between increased use of new technique and labor's

---

4 From 1919 through 1929, net capital formation amounted to $79.1 billion (at 1929 prices). Kuznets, *op. cit.*, p. 269, Table 37. Producers' durable equipment (combined with business construction) constituted about 45 per cent of net capital formation for the same period. *Ibid.*, p. 272.

improved bargaining position. Thus by attaining a higher degree of organization after World War I than ever before, labor was in a position to resist wage cuts during slack periods and to bargain more effectively for wage-rate increases during periods of expansion. Management was confronted with rigidity in that part of the cost structure which generally represents the largest proportion of the total. Attempts to reduce costs in these circumstances might have been expected to take the form of new investment in more productive capital assets.

This is of course only one possible interpretation of the forces behind the sharp upward movement in productivity—the so-called deepening of capital—which took place during the twenties in the United States and continued into the thirties. Other factors beside new capital equipment may account for increased productivity. Changes in the quality of capital equipment replacing depreciated units, improved efficiency in the use of raw materials, and improvement in the quality of goods produced may be other factors contributing to rising productivity.[5] Nonetheless, it seems reasonable to judge the rise in productivity as the result (principally) of a sharp increase in the use of new technique[6] in response to a number of factors of which the most important probably was the strengthening of labor's position as an organized economic group. There is a long-run tendency toward the adoption of improved technique and the reduction of labor-costs apart from the response to wage-rate increases over the short run. An improvement in the bargaining position of labor would seem likely to accentuate this long-run tendency and may be an additional factor inclining business firms toward investment in cost-reducing and labor-saving equipment.

5 *Cf*. Solomon Fabricant, *Output in the Manufacturing Industries*, 1889-1937 (New York: National Bureau of Economic Research, 1940), pp. 16-18.

6 Changes in the composition of new investment indicate an increase in the proportion of producer durable equipment in the sixty-year period from 1869 to 1938, especially in the latter twenty years of the period. *Cf*. Simon Kuznets, *op. cit.*, p. 55.

In any event, the period after World War I seems to have been one of increased emphasis on the substitution of capital for labor (deepening process) in contrast to earlier periods of expansion and increased productivity which took place largely by extending the scale of existing technical facilities (widening process). As Professor Mills puts it,

> In general ... the chief factor in expanding production prior to 1923 was an enlarged body of wage-earners. This was true during the great advances from 1904 to 1909, from 1914 to 1919, from 1921 to 1923. Since 1923, however, better technical equipment, improved organization and enhanced skill on the part of the working force seem definitely to have supplanted numbers as instruments of expanding production.[7]

If the substitution of capital means for labor was the predominant factor in the expansion which took place in the twenties and in new investment during the thirties, then long-term unemployment was closely related to the growth of productive capacity resulting from new investment. The facts are admittedly too complex to be fitted into a simple scheme, though they seem to point in this direction. For one thing drastic reduction in the amount of labor utilized per unit of output was often associated with an aggregate expansion of output, resulting in actual increase in the number of workers

---

7 F. C. Mills, *Economic Tendencies in the United States* (New York: National Bureau of Economic Research, 1932), p. 291. Mills' data show that the notable increase (48 per cent) in output which occurred between 1921 and 1923 was effected with an increase of 30 per cent in the number of workers employed, while the subsequent advance, from 1923 to 1929 saw a marked decline in employment in the industries concerned. Mills estimates that there was a drop of 14 per cent in labor costs between 1923 and 1929. Between 1929 and 1936, principally years of recession, industrial productivity advanced 25 per cent. F. C. Mills, *Prices in Recession and Recovery*, p. 462. Another study of 59 manufacturing industries indicates a rise in productivity of 22 per cent between 1929 and 1936. *Cf.* National Research Project, *Production, Employment and Productivity in 59 Manufacturing Industries, 1919-1936*, Part I, p. 65.

employed.[8] This may have resulted from the effects of new investment or from lowered prices or both.[9] Still, we are discussing long-run developments in the course of which there may have been shorter-run, temporary increases in employment as the income effects (multiplier) and secondary investment (acceleration) effects of new investment ran their course. For another thing, the so-called deepening process which characterized new investment during the twenties and the thirties, may have taken place in response to other factors discussed below, factors which were not unrelated to the displacement of labor by improved technique.

The two factors mentioned—the unstable conditions which confronted new investment, and displacement of labor by improved technique—were closely interrelated during the period. The reduction of labor-costs through investment in new-type facilities may have been a major aim of industrial management under conditions that did not seem to favor adequate returns through the widening process. But continued investment may tend (in time) to yield (more) unused productive capacity and to curtail new investment activity with depressing effects on employment and income. If private capital formation is continued at a high rate nonetheless, it may be because other conditions, say, the price of raw materials and prevailing rates of interest, are favorable. There was in fact a considerable spread between raw material prices and prices of finished goods during the twenties and early thirties.[10] Moreover, inventions

8 Fabricant, *op. cit.*, pp. 18-19. However, earlier data cited by Mills indicate that an increase in productivity of 22 per cent from 1923 to 1929 was attended by a drop of 7.4 per cent in the number of wage earners employed in the industries sampled. F. C. Mills, *op. cit.*, p. 289. The difference between the two sets of facts may result from reference to periods of different duration.

9 On the whole, prices did not go down as new technique was introduced.

10 Mills' data indicate a wider gap between industrial raw materials and manufactured products than existed before World War I; and Mills suggests that this was an important, if not the decisive, factor in the realiza-

may offer profitable opportunities for new investment, as was the case in the twenties and thirties, but only if they provide new fields of entry that are not hedged about by monopolistic restrictions aimed at protecting existing investment in plant and equipment.

A third factor emerges from the interaction of the two which have been discussed. As the scale of investment in new labor-saving equipment rises, the increase in productive capacity is likely to be relatively greater in large-scale firms than in small firms because the large-scale firm with a sizeable wage-bill may find new investment in cost-reducing equipment especially attractive.[11] At the same time the problem of overhead costs is deepened and the need to protect the existing capital structure may be increasingly felt in rigid price and output practices. Improved methods of production — into which much of the capital formation of the twenties and thirties found its way—may lower costs. But it also increases output and tends to depress prices unless a firm can exercise some measure of control over market price. Indeed we find no pronounced downward movement of industrial prices during the period in question. The extension of monopolistic practices—increasing imperfection and restriction of the market—would seem a likely outcome of the growth of productive capacity and the tendency to maintain industrial prices.[12]

---

tion of high profit margins during the twenties. F. C. Mills, *Prices in Recession and Recovery* (New York: National Bureau of Economic Research, 1936), pp. 48, 54, 61 ff., 445.

11 Almost one-half (45 per cent) of net capital formation from 1919 through 1929 consisted of producer durable equipment. Kuznets, *op. cit.* Thus a large portion of new investment found its way into the capital goods sector where firms often operate under conditions of large scale. And, while large-scale production is not necessarily synonymous with monopolistic practice, large-scale firms usually have a history of industrial and financial integration or intra-industry agreements, involving restrictive market practices.

12 That wide-spread elements of imperfect and monopolistic competition are present in the American economy is well known. There is considerable

The three suggested (long-run) dynamic factors—unstable investment conditions, labor displacement due to the adoption of improved technique, and extension of monopolistic practices as the scale of productive capacity rises—are linked in a complex relationship. New capital investment, which was preponderantly channeled into purchases of new and improved equipment in the twenties, increases productive capacity and at the same time results in displacement of labor. Productive capacity is not continually in full use because of measures taken to curtail output and because new investment probably leaves a certain amount of older equipment in use.[13] These circumstances in turn breed conditions in which profitable returns are bound up with investment in new technique, and further displacement of labor, instead of expansion of existing facilities by the widening process.

Monopolistic practices are sometimes regarded as part of a trend in industrial organization intended to lessen uncertainty. Yet restrictions on prices and output tend, among other

difference of opinion, however, as to how seriously competition is affected by these elements. There is no precise way of knowing from the available data. Competition in our industrial society has always been imperfect, but the question at any time is how imperfect. We do know that, of 1807 products, representing more than one-half by value of those included in the Census of Manufactures for 1937, the leading producer accounted for 50 to 75 per cent of total supply in the case of 271 products or more than one-sixth. It is estimated that two-fifths to one-half of the products covered by the census were made in fields in which four concerns controlled three-fourths or more of the supply. See Temporary National Economic Committee, *Competition and Monopoly in American Industry*, pp. 113, 116. We assume here and in what follows that there is substantial concentration and control of the market (oligopoly and monopolistic competition), especially in industries where firms operate under conditions of large-scale and extensive fixed capital investment. There are, of course, wide areas of the economy in which small or medium-sized firms predominate and in which competition is quite active.

13 The tendency to retain older units as newer-type units are purchased might easily result from a policy of trying to recover part of the outlay on new equipment by continuing to take depreciation on older units. At the same time such a policy means retention of a certain amount of unused, less productive capacity.

things, to produce a protected structure which expands along relatively narrow lines, through channels which will reduce labor costs and at the same time will not threaten the capitalized value of the existing structure. New investment would seem to be profitable so long as ability to maintain rigid prices and to curtail output means that the existing capital structure can be safeguarded. The critical point in investment activity may well be reached, however, when benefits to be realized from the purchase of labor-saving equipment may be more than offset by losses which may be sustained on existing (unamortized) capital assets. Of course, control of prices and output means that new capital assets need not compete with existing assets and, in fact, that a rate of return on investments in existing assets may be maintained possibly as a result of savings realized from the use of improved technique. The question of installing newer-type facilities may depend on the actual proportion of older and newer units in use, the relative claims and attitudes of different classes of investors in a firm's capital, and the ability to divert increased earnings (say) from dividends to undistributed earnings.

There is no simple, one-sided relation between new investment and the effects on employment because new investment performs a dual purpose: it increases employment and income at the same time that it increases productive capacity. As one writer has put it, "..... the generation of income and the enlargement of productive capacity often have diametrically opposed effects and the outcome in each particular case depends on the special circumstances involved." [14] In a capitalist economy higher levels of income and employment depend on increased investment. But new investment creates permanent additional capacity at the same time that the income (and secondary investment) effects of a given dose of investment peter out. New investment is needed to maintain employment.

---

14 E. D. Domar, "Expansion and Employment," *American Economic Review*, March, 1947, p. 47.

" But if enough is invested today, still more will be needed tomorrow." [15] And the very process of investment means enlargement of productive capacity and output, pressure on profits, and possibly lessened profitability of some existing capital assets.

THE SHORT-RUN BACKGROUND

The long-term development which has been briefly sketched was not characterized by a smooth, regular growth of output and productive capacity. In fact it would appear that the long-term development of the system of private enterprise cannot be discussed apart from cyclical (and other) fluctuations in employment and output which occur against the background of that development. The long-term movements are marked by repercussions in the shorter run, which in turn may influence the long-range development. The expansion which accompanies new investment activity is the result of a number of conditions connected with the depth and intensity of the preceding recession: the extent to which the scale of capital accumulation has been reduced during the recession; the degree to which costs have been reduced through greater plant efficiency; reorganization of the capital structure; substitution of lower-cost equipment for older equipment; etc. The depth of the recession in turn seems to depend to a considerable extent on the scale of the preceding boom. The extent to which capital values have been increased and resist writing down as earnings fall, the sheer accumulation of capital marking an increase in productive capacity and output in conflict with the aim of restricted output, the growth of overhead charges—all these

15 *Ibid.*, p. 49. This view of investment activity assumes the acceleration principle. As noted earlier Prof. Harrod has examined this relationship in terms of a hypothetical rate of economic growth (" the warranted rate ") deviations from which are self-perpetuating. Lundberg examines the problem in his study on model sequences, and even considers the bearing of long-term investment on the rate of an expansion, i. e. investment which is not dependent on the level of current consumption.

contribute to the problem of liquidation before new investment will again be regarded as profitable.[16]

Alternate up and down movements in business activity may have fairly regular periods because changes in investment may be rather closely geared, with some qualifications, to changes in productive capacity. Thus productive capacity may change qualitatively as a result of technical advance when replacements are made. Here the relative durability of capital plays a leading though not entirely independent role. For other considerations besides the continued efficiency of plant enter into the question of replacement. Under conditions of oligopoly and monopolistic competition better plant may lead to an undesired increase in output or in its quality or both and it is entirely possible that replacements may be postponed when these conditions are present. Productive capacity may also change quantitatively through the addition of new units of equipment. Here the incentive of private gain through capital accumulation asserts itself as a persistent long-term feature of the system of private enterprise. Yet private capital accumulation is subject to forces which make the growth of productive capacity an uneven, jerky affair. In fact the durability of capital and the incentive to accumulate capital would seem to involve conflicts which could lead to cyclical (or other) fluctuations in investment so that the latter become not occasional interludes in the development of a system of private enterprise, but possible stages in that development. The following notes suggest some reasons for the irregularity of investment activity, primarily during the expansion stage, and are not intended as a theory of the cycle.

For one thing the accumulation of capital appears to condition the further growth of productive capacity. As capital assets of a certain type are increased, (say) during a boom,

16 Although the depression of the thirties cannot be taken as final evidence of increasing severity of depression, the fact remains that the factors listed were strong in retarding recovery, and recovery was irregular and marked by unprecedented public investment.

the purchase of additional capital assets means that output produced by older units will have to compete with output produced by newer units. So long as economic activity is at a high level and prices are advancing, this may not be a factor limiting continued (new) investment. Output produced by new units will not force down the price of output produced by older units. In practice, however, obsolescence is going on all the time.[17] In fact some technological improvement usually results when depreciated units are replaced. It would seem reasonable to assume therefore that, as outlays on new equipment are progressively made during an expansion, newer capital units will have technical advantages which older units do not possess. As the scale of capital accumulation mounts during an expansion, this factor—i.e., the obsolescence ratio or ratio of new to old equipment—may impede the purchase of new capital equipment for the following reasons. At a high level of earnings and economic activity existing equipment can be charged off more rapidly. But this is seldom the practice. Unless prices can be increased as a compensating measure or other costs reduced commensurately, the cost of accelerated obsolescence has to be borne by reserves or undistributed profits. And there is a strong tendency not to tamper with reserves or with retained earnings. The rate of new investment—and the boom itself—may be checked in the advanced stages of a boom as the ratio of new equipment to older equipment approaches a limiting value, i.e. when new investment means that a relatively high proportion of existing equipment is rendered obsolete.[18]

17 In the field of public utilities, the Interstate Commerce Commission has noted that: " It is a mistake to assume that inventions or improvements have a sudden effect on an industry. The effect is often quite gradual, in view of the necessity for a period of experimentation, development and preparation for manufacture on a large scale. Past experience also furnishes some gauge of the probable effect of progress in the Art." Quotation by W. A. Paton, *Accountant's Handbook* (3rd ed.; New York: Ronald, 1947), p. 725.

18 Accountants sometimes make a distinction between " gradual " and " sudden " obsolescence, the former being predictable. But they are not

Even routine replacements out of depreciation reserves probably tend to be postponed at this stage for somewhat similar reasons. This may be the point at which new investment involves too high a potential loss on unamortized equipment—at least too high to be recouped quickly by lowered cost of operation—and on the (invested) capital with which the existing equipment has been purchased. It may be the point too at which the cost of older units, not yet recovered through depreciation charges, cannot be readily passed on to higher prices. On the other hand, under conditions of oligopoly or monopolistic competition older units may not be retired simply because the monopolistic firm may be under no compulsion to retire such units and may build up idle capacity by retaining older units even when obsolete. In other words obsolete capital assets, and the investment they represent, are often protected by control over prices and output. Nevertheless, a high proportion of obsolescence does expose the existing capital structure to pressures which probably depend, among other things, on the willingness or ability of management to divert net earnings to surplus or to special reserves as an offset to possible losses. It depends too on the ability to protect output produced with older equipment from possible competition

agreed that efforts should be made to accrue obsolescence as an element in the depreciation allowance. Some accountants, for example, argue that obsolescence should be included in deferred charges, as a loss on retirement, and assigned to succeeding revenues. A related method is to capitalize the loss on retirement as part of the cost of replacement. Others contend that this approach would mean too heavy a burden on the earning power of an improved method, and that the possibility of losses from technical change "is one of the factors which justifies profits." W. A. Paton, *Accountant's Handbook*, p. 734. This point of view is valid in a competitive economy, but hardly tenable in a context where new technique is frequently held back from use because of the possible losses involved on established capital assets. In fact, the indefinite and often contested treatment of obsolescence would seem to indicate that it is a difficult problem made even more difficult possibly by the growth of production capacity under monopolistic conditions. Even if obsolescence were predictable as an element of service life, the point is that the accumulation of obsolescence charges may, during a period of rapid capital expansion, exceed reasonable predictions of service.

offered by products of higher quality produced with improved capital means. Verification of these possibilities needs substantially more empirical evidence than is now available on the depreciation and obsolescence policies of business firms in relation to the rate of technical advance. For reasons suggested below, the rate of discovery of new technique, improved use of raw materials, and technological advance generally may not be the limiting factors sometimes supposed.

Changes in the volume of overhead charges is another, rather closely related, aspect of the problem. During a boom fixed charges tend to rise as the cost of depreciation on additions and replacements mounts and contractural expenses are undertaken and renewed (usually) at rising prices.* This structure may not be burdensome so long as prices for finished goods or the number of units sold are rising. It is quite possible, however, that a growing burden of overhead costs may spell trouble even during the boom and that this factor bears a close causal relationship to the upper turning point of the cycle, especially in the capital goods industries. An expansion in economic activity is not continuous. Seasonal and irregular changes in demand may take place. If there is a period of lowered sales or failure of prices to advance, the burden of overhead charges built up previously, may exert a strong downward pressure on profit-margins and expectations. Small fluctu-

---

* In addition new investment may mean larger fixed capital charges. In the boom following World War II, equity shares were 41 percent of total new issues in 1946, 26 percent in 1947 and about 20 percent in 1948. The shift to bonded indebtedness is partly explained by low interest rates and a consequently widening spread between the cost of financing in securities and bonds. Moreover, the vast growth of institutional savings during the thirties and forties has probably promoted a shift from equity to debt financing. Nevertheless, it should be noted that during the twenties stocks rose above 30 percent of total new security issues in only two years, 1928 and 1929. The highest level reached in the thirties was 33 percent of total new issues in 1937. See U. S. Department of Commerce, Survey of Current Business, March, 1948, Table 4, p. 14. It is true, of course, that securities assume far less importance in financing investment when, as in recent years, investment is financed mainly out of internal funds.

ations in sales may have a pronounced effect on overhead
costs per unit of output and profit-margins. And this factor
may have a cumulative effect on economic activity through
a decline in the rate of new investment. It is true that much
depends on other factors affecting private investment decisions.
Sharply fluctuating overhead costs per unit of output will be
considered by business men in the light of a number of other
conditions existing at a particular time. But the fact remains
that firms possessing a large burden of overhead must consider new investment and plant expansion in relation to charges
which may have to be met out of greatly reduced earnings.
This policy is not restricted to the protection of fixed capital
charges. The claims of invested capital generally, including
dividends, must be considered although perhaps to a lesser
extent. Thus, in commenting on the fact that the steel industry
is a business of wide fluctuations in output and income, Mr.
Irving S. Olds, Chairman of U. S. Steel, has stated:

> It seems to me that if we are going to make a sound corpor-
> ation we must make money in a period like this to accumulate
> funds to take care of a period when operations may be at a
> considerably lower rate. We know that we cannot expect the
> great operating rates of the present time to continue. If the
> operating rate drops to 65 or 75 per cent, a big question mark
> is raised as to where we'll be from the profit standpoint.[19]

While this view may not be typical of all large-scale firms in
the capital goods industries, it may be indicative of the considerations holding back new investment when existing capital
charges and overhead form a high proportion of total costs.
    There is an important qualification which bears on the fore-
going discussion. Large business units are increasingly interested in new and improved methods of production. Research

    19 *New York Times*, April 30, 1947. Since this date, U. S. Steel has an-
nounced price reductions. But its policy on plant expansion still stands.
Similar views have been expressed by Mr. E. M. Voorhees of U. S. Steel,
and by Rufus Tucker of General Motors.

has become an important part of the production process. The possibilities of improved technique and even inventions are not left to chance or to irregular accretion, but are actively investigated by specialized personnel employed by business firms. Yet the restrictions on prices and output exercised by large business firms financially able to conduct research probably mean that the productive possibilities of research results are judged in the first instance by their possible effect on the existing capital structure. Even if the discovery of new technique is regularized through organized research effort by business, new technique is introduced primarily in accordance with the established price and financial policies of business firms.

There is another factor which may influence the timing of the upper turning point of the business cycle, namely observed changes in income concentration during the course of the cycle. In the period from 1918 to 1937 the degree of income concentration increased during periods of business expansion and declined during periods of business contraction.[20] If we assume that the rate of new investment activity

20 Temporary National Economic Committee, *Concentration and Composition of Individual Incomes, 1918-1937*, Monograph No. 4, pp. 17-19. The close correlation between changes in general business activity and changes in the degree of income concentration seems traceable in large part to highly variable income, profits, and losses from the sale of property. Another factor making for cyclical increases in income concentration is changes in dividends, a source of income which is concentrated. *Ibid.*, p. 40. In the present post-war period, changes in income distribution have tended to increase the relative share of middle and lower income groups, thus decreasing the degree of concentration. *Cf. The President's Economic Report,* January 1, 1948, p. 18. The present post-war period, however, is not entirely comparable with the period after World War I, which we have used as our base. First, the present period is too brief for purposes of comparison. Second, some of the factors which may account for the present shifts in the income distribution, e. g., the increased relative share going to farmers, are attributable to special (non-cyclical) factors which were not present in the same degree after World War I, when there was a considerable spread between prices of primary and fabricated materials. Of course, the cyclical tendencies in income distribution which have been cited must be used with caution.

tends to increase as prices rise, then the rate of (net) capital accumulation [21] and productive capacity may grow at a faster rate than consumer purchasing power because income concentration rises concurrently. Since the increase in concentration takes place during the boom, it is not itself the cause of an expansion. But a rise in the degree of income concentration during the boom may speed up the rate of new investment and the growth of productive capacity while consumer purchasing power is increasing at a less rapid rate. If coupled with the factors mentioned above, this factor may possibly have a leading part in determining the timing of the upper turning point.[22] That is, the turning point may come when new investment in productive capacity has increased to a point where the proportion of new to old equipment is relatively high,

---

[21] In practice of course we cannot distinguish readily between new investment and replacements, both of which may increase productive capacity. However, replacements can be (and are) postponed. When replacements are made, they are likely to involve the installation of improved equipment and a higher rate of output. Gross rather than net capital formation is the significant magnitude when we are interested mainly in total capacity; net investment when we are interested in the increment to the total, or the rate of increase of productive capacity.

[22] In short, while greater inequality may stimulate investment activity over the short run through a shift to profits, the result may be that productive capacity and output grow at a relatively faster rate than consumer purchasing power. Income is transferred (say) from consumers to investors through a price rise, i. e., profits (and dividends) increase while real income, and consumer purchasing power, decline. Then, as productive capacity grows and output rises, we have two factors—increased output and lessened purchasing power—which act to bring prices down, not in an orderly adjustment process, but with potent deflationary pressure, curtailment of investment activity and unemployment. This is not identical with the view that a diminishing marginal propensity to consume (psychological law of consumption) results in an increase in savings to a point at which savings exceed available investment outlets. It does suggest that given observed (cyclical) changes in income concentration which prevailed in the past, there may be an increasing gap between the rates of growth of productive capacity and of consumer real income during a boom. In addition, this factor may offer some basis for distinguishing between the effects of changes in real and money wages during expansion and contraction.

overhead costs have risen substantially, and the rate of increase of output has outstripped that of consumer purchasing power concurrent with the growth of income concentration.

THE QUESTION OF INVESTMENT OUTLETS

The problem of securing high and sustained levels of employment over the long run is bound up with the problem of finding profitable outlets for private investment. In what follows the question of investment outlets is examined in the light of the preceding discussion of factors that may govern contemporary investment activity.

The view advanced by Professor Hansen and others that the American economy has reached a stage of maturity—a stage characterized by a dearth of investment outlets—has been ably qualified by A. F. Burns,[23] Professor Ellis [24] and others. There is an aspect of the problem, however, that seems to have received less attention than it deserves. Thus even in the presence of widespread elements of imperfect and monopolistic competition firms are not likely to adapt to the growth of productive capacity by inhibiting new investment entirely. The fact that there may be strong pressure to protect existing investments does not mean that outlets may not be found because the business community will tend to seek such investment outlets, if not at home then abroad. There is a dynamic factor at work, a need for finding profitable investment outlets, that may take a variety of channels.

One possible outlet for new investment under conditions of imperfect competition has been discussed. The main outlet, the one which may yield increased profit-margins with a minimum degree of conflict with existing capital assets [25] is

---

23 Arthur F. Burns, *Economic Research and the Keynesian Thinking of Our Times* (New York: National Bureau of Economic Research, 1946), pp. 12-18.

24 Howard S. Ellis, "Monetary Policy and Investment," *Readings in Business Cycle Theory*, pp. 405-421.

25 There is a fairly obvious distinction between the net earnings of a firm —say, as a percentage of net worth—and the return to equity investors.

investment in more (durable) equipment per unit of output. In fact, the greater the underutilization of capacity, say, as a result of restriction of output, the greater the pressure possibly to seek economies by investment in new and improved technique. But the drawback here is that increased productivity means increased potential output—and displacement of labor. A firm is often able to retain a sizeable part of the benefits of enhanced productivity for itself through control of price and output, and it may even be able to continue amortizing older, less productive units which might be displaced under more competitive conditions. Still the firm achieves an enlarged capacity, perhaps burdens itself with additional capital charges, and even finds that some existing capital assets have been rendered less profitable. The acquisition of improved technique, without benefit of lowered prices, and the concurrent growth of capacity, much of it idle, seem to be significant features of investment activity in our period.

There is another dynamic factor of some importance that is often passed over lightly in discussing the question of available investment outlets. This is the possibility of channeling

---

It is true that the return to equity capital varies somewhat with net earnings. Yet reserves and surplus built-up out of high earnings during a boom are an important source of protection of equity capital, and the profit margin consequently may not always be the best measure of the return which may be expected by equity investors. For example, in the inter-war period (1919-1937) dividends averaged considerably more than 50 per cent of corporate current income annually, dividends being paid out in substantial amounts even when the corporate system was suffering deficits. See Martin Taitel, *Profits, Productive Activities, and New Investment*, T. N. E. C. Monograph No. 12, pp. 43-45. The same source suggests that retained profits of the corporate system during the period 1909-1937 amounted to 35 billion dollars instead of the 9 billion dollars indicated by annual net profit figures. This estimate was based on a comparison of increases in net worth during the period with changes in net equity capital contributions and retained profits, including capital gains. *Ibid.*, pp. 14-15. Kuznets' data indicate an increase in the relative share of dividends in the national income for the period 1929-34, as compared with the preceding five-year period during the twenties. *National Income and Its Composition, 1919-1938*, p. 217.

new investment into foreign areas where it will not compete with the existing capital structure and at the same time will offer advantages in the form of relatively cheap labor supply and raw materials. The thesis advanced by the stagnation theorists to the effect that new territories are no longer available for development does not sound altogether convincing.[26] The foreign investment spree of the twenties may have been unsound in a number of respects and may have been attended by much instability. But it represented a moderate proportion of private U. S. capital formation. The current situation, it is true, poses uncertainties for foreign investment, but the way is being paved for substantial private participation through the U. S. relief and recovery program for Europe. This program of course does not offer the opportunities for investment activity available in earlier periods of development. The European countries are advanced industrial nations, not underdeveloped countries. Nonetheless, success in stabilizing political conditions in Europe is expected to restore the initiative to private investors and may well be followed by activity in other areas, notably Latin America, Africa and, possibly, even the Middle and Far East. Institutions like the International Bank for Reconstruction and Development will assist in the restoration of private investment initiative, both through the investment of funds raised on the capital market and by guarantee of, or participation in, private investment abroad.

Foreign investment activity promises to be an active affair and may provide considerable opportunity for private investment at a high level. Whether it will be sustained is another matter. The growing industrialization of backward areas, coupled with movements for political rights and independence, will bring certain complications. Industrialization and diversification of economies that formerly existed on a backward agriculture, or on the inefficient production of raw materials, may mean increased indigenous demand for primary products,

26 Cf. Hansen, op. cit., pp. 360-361.

as a result of improved living standards and greater need for industrial raw materials. Primary products now produced in backward areas may lose their cheapness. Certainly, native labor will not continue for long to be available for employment at subsistence levels.

Moreover, repayment of capital borrowed from abroad must ultimately be made in goods and services and this in turn means a flow of exports—either from the borrower or a third country—in order to earn necessary foreign exchange. The growth of American investment abroad poses the old problem which has never been answered: will the American economy be able to absorb imports consistently, in amounts enabling borrowers to repay loans? Even if American import volume increases substantially, there is some doubt that countries will allow a sizeable part of their exchange earnings to pass each year to foreign investors. The problem seems to depend in large part on the political factor, on the extent to which backward and underdeveloped countries consolidate as national units, resist the outflow of earnings, and establish practices injurious to private foreign capital.[27]

In short, there seem to be no automatic or purely mechanical tendencies at work in the investment process, such as "oversaving", or a high level of replacement relative to new investment,[28] or a shortage of investment outlets.[29] Instead

27 The question, as to who will assume control of retained earnings, the government or private foreign investors, assumes considerable importance in a period of increasing nationalization and government planning.

28 The facts for the economy as a whole may differ quite substantially from the facts adduced for particular industries or groups of industries. Kuznets' estimates indicate that over the period 1869-78 to 1929-38 the share of net capital formation declined from 15 per cent to 8 per cent. However, if the last two decades are excluded, the decline is from 15 per cent of the national income to a little more than 12 per cent (i. e. for the period 1869-78 to 1919-28). "Setting aside the secular significance of the depression of the 'thirties'" writes Kuznets, "we can say that if a long term decline in the proportion of net capital formation has occurred, it has been quite moderate so far." Kuznets, *National Income: A Summary of the Findings*, pp. 53-54. Kuznets does suggest, however, that there was a re-

possibilities for increasing the rate of return are sought in all directions. The introduction of improved technique and the rise of new industries may be regulated by firms in the interest of controlled output and prices. While this undoubtedly involves restriction of employment and output, it does not mean that substantial industrial progress is at an end.

In conclusion, we might consider the bearing of the foregoing discussion on the causal hypothesis of the boom and upper turning point advanced in the multiplier-acceleration relationship. Instead of a fixed functional relation, it is suggested that complex, non-linear changes take place in the causal sequence. Thus some significant part of current investment seems independent of the current volume of consumption; changes in consumption occur as income concentration rises and real consumer income declines; and the growth of productive capacity may depress profit expectations as returns on older capital units decline and fixed charges mount.

In addition, changes in business confidence must be brought into the picture. While they do govern business confidence over the short run, profit expectations may not be a sufficient basis for judging the reactions of investors and the business community over the long run. We probably have to take account of complicated relations among economic groups which, although reflected somewhat in the changing shares of the national income secured by each of the major functional groups, cannot be studied exclusively in these terms. We must consider,

---

tardation in the rate of growth of durable reproducible wealth (i. e. net stock of construction and equipment)—of the total stock of capital accumulated over the sixty year period, more than one-third was added during the first twenty and much less than one-third during the last twenty.

29 Terborgh's point that "There is no evidence that one 'great new industry' is any more dynamic in its impact on capital formation than ten small industries" seems well taken. George Terborgh, *The Bogey of Economic Maturity* (Chicago: Machinery and Allied Products Institute, 1945), p. 89. It is true that we have many "small" rising industries— aviation, television, plastics, electronics, light metals, etc. However, the question is not one of available investment outlets but of willingness to develop and expand such outlets at the highest possible levels.

for example, the effect on business incentives of public policies which do not merely alter the share of the national income received by different sectors but change the pattern of risk-taking associated with private investment activity. Moreover, the absolute level of investment outlets and the availability of inventions and new technique may be relatively less important than the maintenance of conditions which do not penalize risk-taking. In contemporary conditions the activity of organized economic groups, each tending to view its self-interest differently, thrusts our investigations into new fields of inquiry.

CHAPTER VII
SOME IMPLICATIONS AND CON-
CLUSIONS

EACH of the theories discussed in this study contains aspects of importance to the problem of economic fluctuations. They are not theories of the business cycle, however, nor do they provide us with a complete theory of economic fluctuations, except possibly for the analysis based on a synthesis of the multiplier and the acceleration principle. They are short-run equilibrium theories—with the exception of Swedish theory—and their failure to set forth a self-contained hypothesis of economic fluctuations seems to spring from limitations inherent in equilibrium analysis. By self-contained we mean simply a theory which explains economic fluctuations in terms of forces originating within the economic system, rather than through the intervention of forces outside the system.

What are the alternatives for economic theory? In order to reach significant conclusions in economic inquiry, we need the equipment offered by systematic analysis. Equilibrium analysis represents a body of economic reasoning which has evolved over a considerable period of time. It is accepted by many economists as the most useful theoretical reference point for problems of analysis. The question is what particular purpose does equilibrium analysis serve; what type of theoretical problem does it help us solve? A final word on the equilibrium concept seems to be in place.

A NOTE ON THE EQUILIBRIUM CONCEPT

From an analytical tool intended to develop the main lines of a problem and to simplify the complex forces at work, the notion of equilibrium has come to dominate the conception of events in the real world. When equilibrium analysis is used by economists, the qualifications which must be kept in mind in applying the concept to real problems usually fall away. It

is only in the masterly treatment of the equilibrium method
by a Marshall that we are warned repeatedly that it is an
analytical tool, a method of approximation, to be employed as
a provisional assumption. Marshall seemingly characterized
the generation of economists who followed him when he
wrote: " The Statical Theory of equilibrium is only an introduction to economic studies. . . . . Its limitations are so constantly overlooked, especially by those who approach it from
an abstract point of view, that there is a danger in throwing
it into definite form at all." [1] After Marshall economic theory
for the majority of Anglo-Saxon economists became almost
wholly bound up with equilibrium analysis. Economic theory
came to be concerned with the general problem of how scarce
means are adjusted to alternative ends and the problems subsidiary to this sort of inquiry: the interaction of supply and
demand in reaching an equilibrium price, whether equilibrium
is determinate (i.e. same number of equations as unknowns),
the frictional factors that might prevent adjustments to a new
equilibrium position, etc. The implication of normal stable
positions of rest accompanied this use of the equilibrium concept. Equilibrium analysis was not merely a discipline but
purported to explain persistent tendencies in the real world.
At the same time refinement of the equilibrium method took
the place of new theoretical development in response to changing problems.

Reaction against the equilibrium method has at times been
vigorous, but it has frequently been carried to the point where
economic theory and equilibrium analysis have been treated
as one and the same thing. One of the chief criticisms advanced against economic theory as a result of its long-standing

[1] Alfred Marshall, *Principles of Economics* (8th ed.; New York: Macmillan, 1920), p. 461. Marshall urges caution in the use of the equilibrium
concept at a number of points. *Cf.* pp. 366, f2, 379, f1. The object of economic
inquiry, Marshall tells us, "must be that of living force and movement"
and the static assumptions are used provisionally in order to deal with
forces which are otherwise too numerous. Preface to Eighth Edition, xiv.

association with equilibrium analysis is that theory over-
simplifies the complexities of the real world and that it deals
in relationships which have little but formal significance. The
charge of over-simplification is generally directed at the axioms
of value theory, at the methodological shortcomings of the
theory of exchange or choice, whichever variant is in use, and
at the idealization of economic behavior as rational behavior.
Important as this sort of criticism may be, it seems to bypass
the main issue. Simplification is necessary in developing the
principal lines of a problem because we cannot merely repro-
duce reality and hope to explain anything. The real difficulty,
it would seem, is that economic theory has been held for so
long to a restricted and relatively narrow field of inquiry: the
problem of allocation of scarce resources at the margin and
the determination of equilibrium prices in accordance with
this principle. The formalism of equilibrium analysis does not
spring from the reduction of complex forces to simplified ideas,
but from the character of the inquiry and its hypothesis of
valuation.

This type of inquiry and its various offshoots—quasi-rent,
derived demand, elasticity of demand, factor substitution, opportunity cost, etc.—provide important analytical tools. We
live in a society where individual decisions to buy and sell
goods and services at ruling market prices are a dominant
feature of economic activity. But the supply and demand relations with which equilibrium analysis is concerned tell us only
how a given amount of resources is apportioned over the short
run and how equilibrium is reached at that special set of prices
which equalizes the supply and demand of each commodity in
the economic system.[2] It can tell us little or nothing about the

2 The methodological criticisms which have been directed at equilibrium
analysis need not concern us here. They include such questions as the
validity of the subjective conditions of equilibrium: whether the compatibility
of subjective maximum positions (of utility, profit or income from productive services) reached through marginal allocation has much empirical
meaning.

forces which determine the amount of resources available to the economic community—the incomes realized from selling productive services and from entrepreneurial profits—and how their distribution may possibly affect the economic problem. Income is a given quantity in short-run price-equilibrium analysis. It is the great merit of Keynesian analysis that it concentrates precisely on this feature of the demand-supply relation: the principal forces governing the level of (real) income. But even the General Theory of Employment, as we have seen, does not explain *changes* in the level of income. The latter are dependent on changes in the scale of investment; and this problem falls outside the field of Keynes' short-run analysis. In short, equilibrium analysis is a method which simplifies certain aspects of the economic problem in coherent form; but they are not the aspects which afford an understanding of the outstanding economic questions which concern us today.

The notion of dynamic equilibrium, in contrast to traditional (static) theory, is even more open to question as a concept applicable to the real world. In equilibrium analysis adjustments to new maximum positions (of utility and profit) take place on the assumption that the data and prices are independent of the process of adjustment. For example, as the output of the individual firm increases, the effect (say) on total income payments, or on total resources used in the economy, will ordinarily be negligible. But in the dynamic case changes in data affect large segments of the economy, rather than individual firms and consumers as such. The effect (say) of a change in data and prices is not limited to changes in relative prices but, through the action of money and other liquid assets, extends to changes in the price level. Similarly, the effect of changes in data and prices is not confined to changes in individual outputs but extends to output as a whole. When we are concerned with changes in output as a whole or in the general price level, as we are in the case of dynamic problems, we must reckon with a wide variety of responses by individual firms possessed of different sales, profit, and cost positions.

In saying this, we are asserting, in effect, that monopolistic competition prevails and that firms are unique, rather than identical economic units. An increase in aggregate output and profit is distributed in different amounts among individual firms. In other words we cannot assume that changes in prices and data are followed by adjustments which lead to a unique level of economic activity. Instead, as a result of widely varied responses to such changes, we may find secondary changes in prices and data which result in further adjustments, additional reactions of prices and data, etc. in an indefinite sequence. The upshot is cumulative movement, rather than an unique level of economic activity.

We need not even assume monopolistic competition to make the point. We need only assume, as the Swedish economists do, that changes in prices and data alter business expectations (of profit, costs, sales, etc.) and that this leads to a revision of investment and output plans, thereby altering the level of income. The result is further changes in data and prices which again influence changes in profit expectations. In a dynamic system any given set of changes may start further changes which make it unlikely that the system will come to rest at any particular level of output, prices and employment.

The argument is sometimes advanced in business cycle theory that the concept of equilibrium is needed in order to distinguish fluctuations from the level of economic activity about which they gravitate. Thus it is suggested that empirical measurement of secular trend results in somewhat artificial separation of irregular, cyclical and secular components and leaves considerable uncertainty as to the meaning to be attached to the notion of trend. Since we do not know precisely what statistical trend lines represent, we must make use of concepts which clearly distinguish the " normal " or " going " level of activity from fluctuations about that level. This is more or less the viewpoint of Professor Harrod when he suggests a dynamic equilibrium which is conceived to go on at a required or self-perpetuating rate of growth. " The line of output traced by the warranted rate," says Harrod, " is a moving equilibrium, in the sense that it represents the one level of output at which producers will feel in the upshot that they have done the right thing, and which will induce them to continue in this line of advance." [3] But instability in this type of scheme results in disturbances which are self-aggravating. An excessive output, above the equilibrium rate, results in a deficiency of the actual increase of capital units per unit increment of output relative to that desired. This relative shortage of equipment stimulates further expansion and, the farther that actual output departs from the equilibrium rate of output, the greater the stimulus to expansion.[4]

Another conception of dynamic equilibrium is that of a process taking place over a series of periods, for example, Hicks' temporary equilibrium. The thought behind this approach is that while an equilibrium may not represent persistent relations, an equilibrium is determinate during the period in which it is realized. But if an equilibrium is " temporary ", there is a latent disequilibrium. An indeterminate element in the system becomes apparent at the end of a period when the equilibrium breaks down. Actually, the equilibrium is temporary because expectations, on the basis of which supply and demand commitments are entered into at the beginning of a period, are not compatible. However, the reason for their incompatibility cannot be explained in terms of variations in estimates of the future arising solely from past experience of prices and profits since a substantial part of the uncertainty problem seems to depend on conditions of business confidence and business psychology which are not encompassed in equilibrium analysis. In short, dynamic factors like expectations can be fitted into equilibrium analysis only at the cost of hedging the determinateness of equilibrium.

3 R. F. Harrod, "An Essay in Dynamic Theory," *op. cit.*, p. 22.
4 *Loc. cit.*

There is still another concept of equilibrium, that found in use among some of the Swedish economists, notably Myrdal. This is the concept of monetary equilibrium which, as far as can be judged, has little in common with the traditional (Anglo-Saxon and Walrasian) concept of price equilibrium. It does not imply a position towards which the economic system tends following disturbance. Rather "monetary equilibrium", as viewed by Myrdal, represents a hypothetical "norm" for judging those changes in the economic system which end up in a self-accelerating (cumulative) movement and for suggesting economic policies which may act to check such movements. Apparently no stable position of rest is suggested; only a convenient bench-mark for determining how shifts in profits and production may lead to persistent upward or downward movements.[5] If this is indeed all Myrdal intended by the phrase "monetary equilibrium", the controversy between him and his Swedish colleagues regarding the significance of the concept is hardly important. We may, if we wish, select empirically some set of monetary conditions (i.e. the initial level of savings, investment, and consumption in a given period) which are prior to all others in a cumulative move-

---

5 This concept of "equilibrium" may serve a purpose roughly analogous to the notion of specific and reference-cycle averages worked out by Professors Mitchell and Burns. The latter provide a "norm" against which cyclical movements may be marked and measured. "... what features of a business or specific cycle are 'peculiar', and the way in which they are 'peculiar'," write Mitchell and Burns, "cannot be determined without reference to some 'norm'. Those who accept an episodic theory of business cycles cannot escape having notions of what is 'usual', and what is 'unusual' about any given cycle. By striking averages of cyclical behavior we make such notions more definite." Mitchell and Burns, op. cit., pp. 467-468. Any comparison with Myrdal's concept of monetary equilibrium must, of course, be qualified by the observation that the Mitchell-Burns notion is strictly an empirical affair. The term inductive might be more appropriate because the concept of the reference cycle often depends on reasoning from a variety of scattered evidence, and it involves, too, statistical assumptions which are frequently only hypotheses and not rigidly applicable to observations on economic data.

ment [6] and refer to them as a point of "monetary equilibrium" for purposes of convenience. Yet the term has rather rigid connotations and adds little to the discussion of an accelerating movement when the starting (initial) point of that movement is arbitrarily specified in a sequence analysis.

Consider, finally, one of the features which may be taken as typical of the dynamic problem in contrast to statics: changes in the stock of capital equipment broadly determined by investment decisions. More important, investment is a "lumpy" process because investment activity seems subject to substantial irregularity. It is a process carried on by individual firms without a coordinated plan in the aggregate, indeed in ignorance of the plans of other firms. It is influenced by a number of complicating factors. For example, new investment planned for the purpose of lowering costs must be adjusted to the irregular rate at which new or improved methods make their appearance. Again, firms in an industry and different industries have investment programs corresponding to different stages of growth and decline. Still another factor is the existing accumulation of capital which varies among firms and industries and results in investment patterns of different timing and intensity. Firms may hesitate to increase their capital investment because output produced with existing equipment will have to compete with output produced by new, possibly improved methods. Under monopolistic conditions the tendency, which is frequently present, to protect the valuation of existing investment until fully amortized often acts to reduce the amount of new investment. We may speak then of an irregular investment process which can generate changes in income levels, employment and prices quite apart from the forces considered in traditional analysis, a process, in fact,

6 The only difficulty here is that the judgment as to what comes first must be rather arbitrary. Should we start (say) with conditions at the bottom of the recession, if we are tracing the beginning of an expansion, or some intermediate point?

which may impose oscillations on the rest of the economic system.

In conclusion, the idea of moving equilibrium does not seem to fit the kind of changes which occur under dynamic conditions. When an equilibrium is regarded as unstable and possibly indeterminate, when it is prone to cumulative disturbance and irregular alteration, we can no longer assume a " normal " line of advance and occasional departures from " normal ". Neither can we substitute the idea of dynamic equilibrium for the complex process of change and growth that characterizes our economic system. The fact that observed (cyclical and irregular) fluctuations about the secular trend cannot be disentangled from trend suggests that growth in our economic system may be typically irregular and jerky and, possibly, that short-term fluctuations and the more marked cyclical movements represent particular stages of growth (or decline) in which the unevenness of economic development is aggravated and becomes more apparent. Indeed, it seems inevitable that, with the development of dynamic economics, the relevance of the equilibrium concept should be called into question and its limitations sharply exposed.

Economic Fluctuations and the Dynamic Problem

New investment is the force on which the system of private enterprise thrives. Yet, though the generation of employment and income is dependent on continued (new) investment, the latter is governed by conditions which make it unlikely that investment will be a sustained process. Thus enlargement of productive capacity appears to have a complex effect on the rate of investment, especially in industries where monopolistic or imperfect competition prevail. As capacity grows, the main path of adjustment seems to lie in investment, at home and abroad, which is not competitive with established capacity and the capital structure which goes with it. And new investment under monopolistic conditions, can be rendered non-competitive with established plant up to a point. This sort of adjustment may entail (more) idle capacity and lessened profitability per unit of output leading to further investment in labor-saving equipment and cost-reducing technique, etc. Thus when, under monopolistic conditions, capacity is not in full use, it may be preferable to increase returns (per unit of output) by decreasing costs through investment in improved technique, rather than to increase the number of units of output. We have a process in which attempts to increase the rate of return (per unit) by investment in improved technique offers the main path of adjustment and yet builds up capacity which cannot be used profitably.

Changes in employment in these circumstances seem to be bound up with cyclical and irregular changes in the level of productive capacity and output; and long-term changes which alter the conditions under which new capacity may be profitably employed. The view, which is best represented by the theory based on a synthesis of the multiplier and acceleration principle, that the level of investment activity depends on the demand for finished goods, does not fully explain cyclical changes in income and employment. The question is where does an initial stimulus to demand come from? New investment, following, say, upon a period of slow depreciation of capital assets and net disinvestment during the depression, may generate income in the familiar multiplier effect. Increased income in turn may increase demand and lead to additional investment. But once the income and accelerator effects of a dose of new investment has dwindled, what sustains new investment? The answer seems to lie in the complex interaction of long-run and short-run factors, rather than exclusively in short-run cumulative movements flowing from new investments, increased income and demand, and new derived investment. As an example, we may note that, in the depression which commenced in 1929, there was substantial increase in productivity based on investment in improved technique. At the same time there was no pronounced retirement of older units. Depression did not lead to a sloughing off of capacity through retirement of older units, and the business practices generally followed were in line with the long-run development of productive capacity under controlled conditions of prices and production.

In addition, we find evidence of fluctuations in income, including shifts in the distribution of income at different stages in the cycle—toward a lesser concentration in the recession and a higher concentration in the boom. Investment activity over the short run may parallel these changes in income concentration. For example, a boom may come to an end when new investment has proceeded to a point at which the proportion of new to older instruments of production is high and displacement by new, improved equipment becomes increasingly unprofitable; the overhead burden is large and sensitive to fluctuations per unit of output; and the rate of growth of productive capacity and output tend to outstrip that of consumer purchasing power as (relative) income inequality increases.[7] Changes in the rate of growth of consumer demand are probably an important factor in the timing of the upper turning point. But such changes perhaps act as a reinforcing factor, not as the main variable governing investment activity. It might be most useful to know, for example, how an expansion affects real income and expenditure. Does the elasticity of demand for different kinds of consumer goods vary sufficiently so that rising prices tend to divert expenditure from certain categories of consumer goods to others? In other words, what are the relatively rigid elements in consumer expenditure? If expenditures on consumer durable goods tend to be postponed

7 In short, while higher income concentration may stimulate investment activity, the result may be that productive capacity and output grow at a faster rate than consumer income. Higher income concentration during a boom is in part a result of increased profits (i. e. dividends) and capital gains and in part a consequence of rising prices. For capital gains are closely associated with price expansion and are largely received by those with higher incomes. *Cf.* Temporary National Economic Committee, *Monograph No. 4,* p. 39.

as prices rise during a boom, then the effect of price expansion, and changes in real income, may induce shifts in consumer demand. And these changes in consumer demand as prices rise —consisting (say) of a shift from durable to " cost-of-living " items—might explain a drop in investment activity without reference to a diminishing marginal propensity to consume. The relation between changes in real and money income during an expansion, including the effects on income concentration and changes in the type of consumer demand, remains one of the more obscure but promising areas of investigation in business cycle study.

The second factor—changes in the conditions under which new productive capacity may be profitably employed—yields the possibility of chronic long-run unemployment. The statistical evidence, at least in terms of long-run shifts in the distribution of national income, is not conclusive.[8] The strong bargaining position of organized labor, able to resist pressure on wage-income over the long run, has undoubtedly lessened encroachment on the income share of wage-earners after World War I. Moreover, the relatively poor bargaining position of primary producers up to World War II probably provided a cushion which kept the share of wage-income fairly stable in the face of long-run under-utilization of productive capacity.

These factors might account for the fact that the share of wage-earners in the national income has remained relatively stable despite controlled prices and restrictive output practices in a number of strategic fields. But the positions of different economic groups are not final or permanent. What adjustments will follow as the pressure on profit margins mounts, a pressure inherent in the growth of productive capacity under conditions of under-utilization and rigid prices? Unless prices decline over the long run, expenditures on capital assets will

8 See the data cited by M. Kalecki in support of the thesis of relative income stability (manual workers), for the period 1919-1935, *Essays in the Theory of Economic Fluctuations* (New York; Farrar, 1939).

have to grow at an increasing rate in order to generate a level of income commensurate with the growth of productive capacity. However, so long as investment activity is geared to the protection of existing productive capacity and the maintenance of rigid prices in a number of fields, national income, except for exceptional post-war conditions, is likely to lag behind full use of capacity. In a word, we are likely to have underemployment and a decline in the relative share of wage-income over the long run under the conditions mentioned.

There are indications too that raw materials will not be available on the favorable terms possible before World War II. Backward areas are intent on industrialization and private investment opportunities in colonial areas, with some exceptions, are diminishing rapidly under altered political conditions. Will private investment at home continue to take the form of investment in labor-saving and cost-reducing equipment as the best source of enhanced profitability? Or will new methods of investment, undertaken under state guidance and guarantee, provide profitable outlets for private investment for some time to come? Only the future will tell.

It cannot be denied that theory should confine itself to matters which can be systematically analyzed and specifically related to economic activity instead of losing itself in a welter of possible relationships. The theory of employment, however has supplied us with tools which may enable us to go far beyond traditional price analysis. In the concept of effective demand we have a far-reaching qualification of traditional value theory: full employment of resources—reached automatically in conventional theory through equivalence of marginal utilities in the allocation of productive factors—is a special (limiting) case; and the level of employment depends (essentially) on the state of investment decisions. Above all, the theory of employment has given us an analysis of income flow to different groups in the community whose interests, in disposing of income received, may diverge considerably. It is true that this theory does not deal with the long-run effect on investment activity of changes in productive capacity and the adjustments made by different income groups to such changes. These adjustments are in part a response to the state of prices and the existing level of productive capacity, and in part a response to the relations existing between the business community and other income groups—wage-earners, producers of raw materials and even groups within the business community itself. To understand investment activity it seems that we need to trace the process of economic adjustment back to these reactions and relationships, instead of studying the effects alone as they are expressed in prices, investment decisions and changes in the rate of growth of productive capacity.

Consider what this implies for the theory of economic fluctuations and such subsidiary questions as the formation of expectations and business confidence. The notion of " confidence " is frequently mentioned in contemporary theories of economic fluctuations. But most of the theories which make use of this concept view it as the product of estimates of future prices (or profits) by individuals (firms or households) based on " economic " experience of the present and recent past. The question of " confidence " or " lack of confidence ", as suggested earlier, is a much broader issue, one that cannot be adequately explained within the framework of equilibrium analysis and price theory proper. Generally speaking, the term confidence in the current literature on expectations embraces certain factors which may affect the stability of prices and investments. Since the purchase of capital goods involves a long-term commitment to keep assets in illiquid form, investors will part with liquidity for shorter or longer periods, and business men will undertake an expansion of capacity and output, depending on their appraisal of the forces making for stability or lack of stability. But these groups can make only partial estimates of the future because many of the factors entering into their estimates are unpredictable. Business estimates of the future might involve appraisal of prices in the immediate and more remote past, the state of current demand and supply conditions, government fiscal policy, the possibility of technological change, the bargaining position of unions, the possibility of adverse or favorable political changes, etc. While all these factors may influence the view taken regarding the stability of investments, they are not entirely calculable over the short run because they shade off into a more or less distant future. In fact, uncertainty of the future seems to entail long-run forces which cannot be estimated by business men or investors in anything but the roughest terms. Since these forces are not reducible to strict mathematical calculation (i.e., probabilities), investment activity seems subject to sudden unforeseen change in the short-run theories which attribute economic fluctuations primarily to changes in expectations.

Moreover, theories which explain business fluctuations in terms of changing expectations all too often assume that the factors which deter or stimulate private enterprise are a simple function of estimated chances of profitability based on experience of the recent past. But business men and investors do not merely calculate their chances of profitability and arrange their plans accordingly. Rather, they often actively intervene in the economic process, in part perhaps to narrow the degree of uncertainty, whether through organization of the market, or by technological adjustments, or by attempting to influence the formation of public policy and so on. The concept of passive adjustment to changes in the data and prices has been substantially revised in the theory of price under conditions of oligopoly and monopolistic competition. A similar revision of theory seems overdue with respect to the activities of organized economic groups as they affect investment activity and employment.

It is a commonplace that relations among different economic groups are often closly reflected in the field of public policy. The state is not an impersonal machine set off apart from its human participants, but a force which mirrors deep-seated institutional and property relations. Yet the activity of economic groups in the formation of public policy is a field of

study which has been shunned by economic theorists in their
capacity as theorists. The task of analyzing these relations has
been left to political scientists, economic historians and sociolo-
gists. Perhaps the fault lies in the present tendency toward
specialization and the division of subject matter into compartments. Certainly equilibrium analysis, which has confined
economic theory to the problem of allocation at the margin,
bears its share of the blame for the cleavage between economic
theory and economic policy. The predominance of equilibrium
analysis made it possible in the past to label some matters as
" economic " and others, including public policy and group
interests, as " non-economic ". The justification usually given
for such reasoning has been that economic theory should en-
compass only those factors which involve the determination
of price-equilibrium and that, in the interest of exact analysis
of this problem, the area of economic inquiry has to be
severely limited.

The study of public policy as exemplified in tariff legislation,
tax legislation and government expenditure adds substantially
to our understanding of relations among economic groups.
Similar possibilities exist in the field of industrial relations
and labor and wage policy. While there is a wealth of information available on these subjects, they have been compart-
mentalized, under the headings of trade policy, or fiscal policy,
or labor economics, as independent fields of study having a
rather vague connection with the main variables governing
investment and employmen. The problems of our day seem to
call for an advance in theory which can explain how the changing fortunes and relations of strategic economic groups influence the determinants of investment and employment.

There is, of course, more to the problem than this. Contemporary economic theory seems to be caught between two
distinct types of analysis: the traditional value problem framed
in terms of " rational " individual conduct in maximizing returns from scarce resources; and the problem of dynamic
change in the economy as a whole. When we examine such

concepts as output as a whole, or investment and consumption for the economy at large, we come up short against the fact that aggregate concepts are deficient by the standards of traditional theory. On the one hand, we are concerned with the variety of individual reactions to changing data, reactions which make it appear that aggregates conceal the true picture of forces governing economic action in a system of private enterprise. On the other, we find it necessary to know more about processes which affect the economy as a whole, processes which govern cumulative expansion or contraction, cyclical swings and the long-term growth of the system. That the distinction exists and that it troubles contemporary theorists is evident in the attempts that have been made to reconcile so-called micro- and macro-economic analysis, i.e., the analysis of individual-behavior and that of particular economic groups having certain characteristics in common. Professor Marschak voices the dilemma when he writes,

> There exists, in fact, an awkward gap: that between the theorems which the undergraduate is taught to derive from the rational behaviour of single firms and consumers ... and the rather crude and sudden assumptions of the macro-discussion on, say, ' investments as a whole ' ... [9]

But the dilemma, if it is indeed that, may exist only because we continue to view problems that affect the economy as a whole from the standpoint of a theoretical apparatus concerned with " rational " individual conduct in the formation of particular prices. Consider, for example, the implications of business contraction under conditions of uncertainty. From the standpoint of the individual firm in traditional value theory such adjustments may be eminently rational in terms of profit maximization. From the viewpoint of the community at large they may be economically undesirable because they result in

9 J. Marschak, "A Cross Section of Business Cycle Discussion ", *American Economic Review*, June, 1945, p. 376.

waste and unemployment. Evidently, the rational behavior of firms in the traditional sense may be a poor criterion to apply to the economy at large. When we shift our attention to the world as it is, when we pass from the conception of purely competitive factors interchangeable as equivalents at the margin to that of institutional groups occupying varying positions of economic power, we require a different type of theoretical apparatus. Indeed with the advent of the theories of employment and imperfect competition we seem to find ourselves in a transitional phase of economic thought as great perhaps as that which began toward the close of the eighteenth century and one in which there is discernable a similar groping toward a new theoretical structure.

BIBLIOGRAPHY

The American Economic Association. *Readings in Business Cycle Theory*. Philadelphia: The Blakiston Co., 1944.

Anderson, Oskar, "The Logic of Decomposition of Time Series," *Journal of the Royal Statistical Society*, XC (1927).

Burns, Aruther F., *Economic Research and the Keynesian Thinking of Our Times*. New York: National Bureau of Economic Research, 1946.

——. "Keynesian Economics Once Again," *Review of Economic Statistics*, XXIX (1947).

——. With Wesley C. Mitchell. *Measuring Business Cycles*. New York: National Bureau of Economic Research, 1946.

Clark, John Maurice. *Strategic Factors in Business Cycles*. New York: National Bureau of Economic Research, 1934.

——. "Additional Note on Business Acceleration and the Law of Demand," *Readings in Business Cycle Theory*.

——. "Capital Production and Consumer-Taking: A Further Word," *Journal of Political Economy*, XL (1932).

Domar, E. D., "Expansion and Employment," *American Economic Review*, XXXVII (1947).

The Economic Report of the President. Washington: U. S. Government Printing Office, January 1, 1948.

Ellis, Howard S., "Monetary Policy and Investment," *Readings in Business Cycle Theory*.

Ezekiel, Mordecai, "Savings, Investment and Consumption: I," *American Economic Review*, XXXII (1942).

——. "Saving, Investment and Consumption: II," *American Economic Review*, XXXII (1942).

Fabricant, Solomon. *Output in the Manufacturing Industries*. New York: National Bureau of the Economic Research, 1940.

Fisher, R. A. *Statistical Methods for Research Workers*, 9th ed. London: Oliver, 1944.

Frisch, Ragnar. *Statistical Confluence Analysis by Means of Complete Regression Systems*. Oslo: Institute of Economics, 1934.

——. "On the Notion of Equilibrium and Disequilibrium," *Review of Economic Studies*, III (1936).

——. "Propagation and Impulse Problems in Dynamic Economics," *Economic Essays in Honor of Gustav Cassel*.

Goodwin, Richard M., "The Multiplier," *The New Economics*. New York: Knopf, 1947.

Graham, Frank D., *Social Goals and Economic Institutions*. Princeton: Princeton University Press, 1942.

Haavelmo, Trygve. "The Probability Approach in Econometrics," *Econometrica*, XII, Supplement (1944).

Haberler, Gottfried. *Prosperity and Depression*, 3rd ed. New York: Columbia University Press, 1941.

——. " Mr. Keynes' Theory of the Multiplier," Readings in Business Cycle Theory, 195 ff.

Hansen, Alvin H. *Fiscal Policy and Business Cycles.* New York: Norton, 1941.

Harrod, R. F. *The Trade Cycle.* Oxford: Oxford University Press, 1936.

——. "An Essay in Dynamic Theory," Economic Journal, XLIX (1936).

——. " Mr. Keynes and Traditional Theory," Econometrica, V, 1936.

Hart, Albert G., "Anticipations, Business Planning and the Cycle," Quarterly Journal of Economics, LI (1937).

Hicks, John R. *Value and Capital,* 1st ed. Oxford: Oxford University Press, 1939.

——. "A Suggestion for Simplifying the Theory of Money," Economica, II, new series (1935).

——. " Mr. Keynes' Theory of Employment," Economic Journal, XLVI 1936).

Kalecki, Michael. *Essays in the Theory of Economic Fluctuations.* New York: Farrar, 1939.

Keynes, John Maynard. *The General Theory of Employment, Interest and Money.* New York: Harcourt Brace & Co., 1936.

——. " General Theory of Employment," Quarterly Journal of Economics, LI (1937).

Kuznets, Simon. *National Income and its Composition, 1919-1938.* New York: National Bureau of Economic Research, 1944.

——. *National Income, A Summary of the Findings.* New York: National Bureau of Economic Research, 1946.

——. " Equilibrium Economics," Quarterly Journal of Economics, XLIV (1930).

——. " Relation Between Capital Goods and Finished Goods," Economic Essays in Honor of Wesley Clair Mitchell. New York: Columbia University Press, 1935.

Lange, Oskar. *Price Flexibility and Employment.* Bloomington: Principia Press, 1944.

Lerner, Abba P., " Some Swedish Stepping Stones in Economic Theory," Canadian Journal of Economics and Political Science, VII (1941).

Lindahl, Erik. *Studies in the Theory of Money and Capital.* New York: Farrar, 1940.

Lundberg, Erik. *Studies in the Theory of Economic Expansion.* New York: King, 1937.

Makower, H. and Marschak, J., "Assets, Prices and Monetary Theory," Economica, new series (1938).

Marschak, Jacob. "A Cross Section of Business Cycle Discussion," American Economic Review, XXXV (1945).

——. " Lack of Confidence," Social Research, VIII (1941).

Marshall, Alfred. *Principles of Economics,* 8th ed. New York: MacMillan, 1920.

Metzler, Lloyd A., " Keynes and the Theory of the Business Cycle," The New Economics.

——. "Stability of Multiple Markets: The Hicks Conditions," Econometrica, XIII (1945).

Mills, Frederick C. *Economic Tendencies in the United States*. New York: National Bureau of Economic Research, 1932.

——. *Prices in Recession and Recovery*. New York: National Bureau of Economic Research, 1936.

Mitchell, Wesley C. *Business Cycles*. Berkeley: University of California Press, 1913.

——. *Business Cycles, The Problem and Its Setting*. New York: National Bureau of Economic Research, 1927.

——. With Burns, A. F. *Measuring Business Cycles*.

Myrdal, Gunnar. *Monetary Equilibirium*. London: Hodge, 1939.

Ohlin, Bertil, "The Stockholm Theory of Savings and Investment," Readings in Business Cycle Theory.

Paton, W. A. *Accountant's Handbook*, 3rd ed. New York: Ronald, 1947.

Pigou, A. C., "Mr. Keynes' Theory of Employment, Interest and Money," Economica III, new series (1936).

Ricardo, David. *The Principles of Political Economy and Taxation*. New York: Dutton & Co., 1911.

Robertson, Dennis H., "Review of the Trade Cycle by R. F. Harrod," Canadian Journal of Economics and Political Science, III (1937).

——. *Money*. Harcourt Brace & Co., 1922.

Robinson, Joan. *Essays in the Theory of Employment*, 2nd ed. New York: MacMillan & Co., 1948.

Rosenstein-Rodan, P. N., "The Coordination of the General Theory of Money and Price," Economica, III, new series (1936).

Samuelson, Paul A., "Interaction between the Acceleration Principle and the Multiplier," Review of Economic Statistics, XXI (1939).

——. "The Stability of Equilibrium: Comparative Statics and Dynamics," Econometrica, IX (1941).

Schumpeter, Joseph A. *Business Cycles*, I. New York: McGraw-Hill, 1939.

——. *The Theory of Economic Development*. Cambridge: Harvard University Press, 1934.

Temporary National Economic Committee. *Competition and Monopoly in American Industry*. Washington: U. S. Government Printing Office, 1940.

——. *Concentration and Composition of Individual Incomes, 1918-1937*. Washington: U. S. Government Printing Office, 1941.

——. *Profits, Productive Activities, and New Investment*. Washington: U. S. Government Printing Office, 1941.

Terborgh, George. *The Bogey of Economic Maturity*. Chicago: Machinery and Allied Products Institute, 1945.

Tinbergen, Jan. Statistical Testing of Business Cycle Theories, I. *A Method and Its Application to Investment Activity*, II, *Business Cycles in the U. S. A. 1919-1932*. Geneva: League of Nations, 1930.

——, "Econometric Business Cycle Research," Readings in Business Cycle Theory.

Wicksell, Knut. *Lectures on Political Economy*, II. London: Routledge, 1935.

Wright, Chester. *Economic History of the United States*. New York: McGraw-Hill, 1941.

INDEX

Acceleration principle, 10, 64-65, 82-83; and multiplier, 109-114, 119, 143-144; qualifying assumptions, 116-117
Anticipations, 43-44, 54

Burns, A. F., 87, 119, 139
Business confidence, 53, 55-57, 158; See: Expectations; Theory of money

Cannan, E., 21
Clark, J. M., 19, 64, 83-84, 110, 117
Consumption function, 109-110, 115; stability of, 118; See: Acceleration principle
Corn Laws, 90
Cumulative process, 12-13, 46, 60-64, 148-149; See: Economy at large

Domar, E., 64, 130-131
Durability of Capital, 108, 120, 132-135

Econometric analysis, 27-30, 32-33, 79-87; See: Random factors; "Shock" theory; Model analysis
Economy at large, 12-13, 31, 67-69, 148-149; and micro-analysis, 160-162
Ellis, H. S., 139
Equilibrium: as causal relation, 35-39; determinate, 12, 32, 37-38, 57; disturbance of, 14, 29, 33, 35, 39, 46; in Swedish analysis, 73, 151-152; in traditional theory, 15, 145-147; and short-run analysis, 32-33, 98, 102, 147-148; temporary, 42-58; under dynamic conditions, 12-14, 59-60, 72-75, 148-153; See: Expectations; Model analysis
Expectations, 14, 31, 33; as probability estimates, 52-53; and business confidence, 53-56, 158; and economic fluctuations, 14, 107, 121, 145, 158-159; incompatibility of, 73, 150; in traditional analysis, 42-44; Keynes' treatment of, 99-102
Ezekiel, M., 116, 118

Fabricant, S., 125
Fisher, R. A., 85, 87

Frisch, R., 28-29, 75, 82-85
Functional scheme, 35-36, 88-89, 122; See: Model analysis; Probability theory

Goodwin, R. M., 109
Graham, F. D., 39

Haavelmo, T., 27, 85-86
Haberler, G., 75, 109, 116
Hansen, A. H., 109, 113, 114-115, 118, 139, 141
Harrod, R. F., 15, 23, 30, 64, 105, 109, 111-113, 130, 149-150
Hart, A. G., 54
Hawtrey, R. H., 21
Hayek, F., 21
Hicks, J. R., 21-22, 31-32, 44, 45-52, 59, 71-73, 76-77, 93, 150
Historical process, 90, 104
Hurwicz, L., 87

Income distribution: during boom, 137, 158; and investment activity 137-138, 156-158; over long run, 163-104, 143-144, 156-157
Interstate Commerce Commission, 133
Investment activity, 102-103, 116, 118-119, 153-158; and deepening process, 125-127, 129-130, 140, 153-154; dynamic changes in, 64-65, 70-71, 106-107, 115, 132, 139-144, 152-153; and fiscal policy, 121, 143-144, 160; foreign, 123, 140-142, 157; in U. S. economy, 122-125, 128, 135-136, 142-143; restriction of, 105, 129-130, 137, 139-140, 152, 157; stability of, 99-102, 132, 152, 158-159

Jevons, W. S., 17
Joplin, T., 21
Juglar, C., 17

Kalecki, M., 64, 156
Keynes, J. M., 13, 22-25, 31-32, 43, 59, 71, 91 ff., 148
Koopmans, T., 27, 84
Kuznets, S., 117, 118, 123, 140, 142

Lange, O., 21, 72
Langton, W., 17

Lavington, F., 20
Lederer, E., 18
Lerner, A. P., 59
Lindahl, E., 21, 25, 61, 62, 72, 80
Loewe, A., 18, 40
Lundberg, E., 25, 64-65, 78

Makower, H., 43
Malthus, T. R., 16, 17, 21
Marginal efficiency of capital, 23-24, 65, 95, 98; long-run influences on, 102-105; and turning points, 107-108
Marschak, J., 43, 53, 161
Marshall, A., 17, 146
Marx, K., 17
Metzler, L. A., 74, 110
Mill, J. S., 17
Mills, F. C. 126, 127-128
Mills, J. 17
Mitchell, W. C., 18, 19, 55-56, 87
Model analysis, 30-31, 81, 84, 87-90, 122; See: Econometric analysis
Monetary stability, 30-31
Money, theory of, 11-14, 20-21, 30-32, 43-44, 55, 58, 93, 96; See: Expectations
Myrdal, G., 63, 73, 77, 151

Neyman—Pearson hypothesis, 85
New or improved technique, 100, 127-128, 130, 135, 137, 14⌐ .44, 152, 154; See: Investment ⌐ivity
"Non-economic" forces, ⌐1, 101, 160; See: Equilibriu⌐ ⌐nalysis

Obsolescence, 133-1 ⌐
Ohlin, B., 25, 30⌐ ⌐, 59, 73
Olds, J. S., ⌐ 136
Overhead c' ⌐ges, 128, 139, 155; in boom, ⌐ ⌐-136

Pato⌐ W. A., 133, 134
Per⌐ ⌐d analysis, 63-64, 66-71, 78
Pigou, A. C., 97-98
Prices, in temporary equilibrium analysis, 46-47, 49-51, 54; rigid prices, 124, 125, 127-128, 130, 157; of primary products, 127, 142, 157; See: Expectations
Probability, theory of, 36, 88-89; restrictions in application to time series, 38, 84-85, 88-90; sample

points, 86; unforseen changes in, 99-100, 102, 158-159; See: Expectations; Random factors; Model analysis
Productivity in U. S., 126, 127
Public Policy, 121, 159-160; and economic groups, 143-144, 162

Random factors, 29, 30, 33, 80-85, 87-89; See: Econometric analysis; Model analysis
Retained earnings, 130, 134, 135, 139-140
Ricardo, D., 16, 17
Robertson, D. H., 39, 116
Robinson, J., 57
Rosenstein-Rodan, P., 20, 43

Samuelson, P. A., 72, 109, 113-114
Smith, A., 17
Schumpeter, J. A., 18, 40-42, 83
Self-contained analysis, 14, 41, 52, 58, 121, 122, 145; See: Equilibrium; Model analysis
"Shock" theory of business cycle, 29, 82-85; See: Frisch; Clark
Speeds of reaction, 26-27, 68, 76-77, See: Stability conditions
Stability conditions, 72, 74-75
Stabilizers, 49-50
Substitution, intertemporal, 22, 46; of capital for manpower, 124-127, 140, 154

Taitel, M., 140
Terborgh, G., 143
Thornton, H., 21
Tinbergen, J., 27, 59, 80, 81, 82, 84
Traditional theory, 15-16, 37-40, 93, 145-148, 160-162; See: Equilibrium
Tucker, R., 136
Tugan—Boranowski, M. J., 17

Uncertainty, 13, 42, 44, 52-53

Veblen, T., 16, 18
Vorhees, E. M., 136

Walras, L., 20, 21
West, E., 16
Wicksell, K., 18, 60-63, 76, 83
Wright, C., 123